TRAVELLING THE SANDS

Andrew Taylor's childhood was spent in his native Yorkshire where his parents, both teachers, encouraged his child's curiosity for what lay over the next hill. After taking a degree in English, he opted for a career in journalism. He worked for the *Daily Express* and BBC Television News before moving to Dubai Television in 1988.

During his five years as a reporter and news editor in Dubai, he contributed articles about the Gulf to many publications, including *The Times, Sunday Telegraph* and *Spectator*.

In the course of his reporting he developed a fascination with the history of Arabia which led him to seek out the original texts written by the great explorers, many of them now out of date and out of print. This book combines these researches with his journalistic flair for a good story.

Andrew Taylor currently works as a journalist in London. He lives in Oxfordshire with his wife and three children.

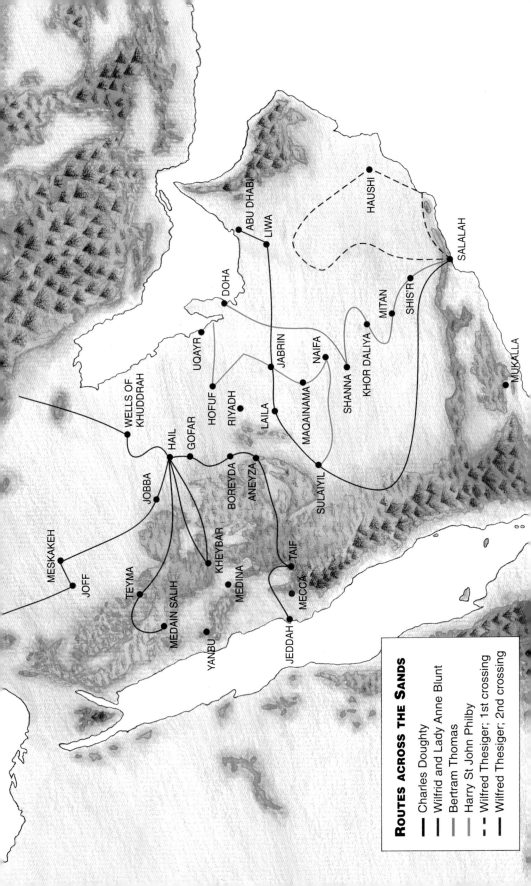

ROUTES ACROSS THE SANDS

— Charles Doughty
— Wilfrid and Lady Anne Blunt
— Bertram Thomas
— Harry St John Philby
-- Wilfred Thesiger; 1st crossing
— Wilfred Thesiger; 2nd crossing

ABU DHABI
LIWA
HAUSHI
SALALAH
DOHA
SHIS'R
MITAN
KHOR DALIYA
MUKALLA
UQAYR
JABRIN
NAIFA
SHANNA
WELLS OF
KHUDDRAH
HOFUF
MAQAINAMA
HAIL
GOFAR
RIYADH
LAILA
SULAIYIL
JOBBA
BOREYDA
ANEYZA
MESKAKEH
JOFF
KHEYBAR
TAIF
TEYMA
MEDINA
MECCA
MEDAIN SALIH
YANBU
JEDDAH

Travelling
the
SANDS

Sagas of Exploration in the
Arabian Peninsula

Andrew Taylor

MOTIVATE
PUBLISHING

Published by Motivate Publishing

Dubai: PO Box 2331, Dubai, UAE.
Tel: 2824060, Fax: 2824436, E-mail: motivate@emirates.net.ae
Abu Dhabi: PO Box 43072, Abu Dhabi, UAE. Tel: 6271666, Fax: 6271888
London: Stewart's Court, 220 Stewart's Road, London SW8 4UD
Tel: (44) 020 7627 2481, Fax: (44) 020 7720 3158

Directors: Obaid Humaid Al Tayer and Ian Fairservice

First published 1995
First softback edition 1997
Reprinted 1998
Third printing 2000

© 1995 Andrew Taylor and Motivate Publishing

ISBN 1 86063 058 8

British Library Cataloguing-in-Publication Data. A catalogue record for this
book is available from the British Library.

Printed by Emirates Printing Press, Dubai

CONTENTS

The Challenge of the Desert

"Would but the Desert of the Fountain yield
One glimpse — if dimly yet indeed revealed
To which the fainting traveller might spring
As springs the trampled herbage of the field."
— Edward Fitzgerald, 'The Rubaiyat
of Omar Khayyam'

For centuries, the two hundred thousand square miles of desert at the heart of Arabia were unknown and unexplored. The travelling bedu who lived on the fringes of the sands may have wandered over parts of them in their endless search for grazing and food, but if ever any of the tribesmen crossed them from side to side, either by accident or in a spirit of adventure, they left no maps and no accounts of their travels.

Right into the twentieth century, the Empty Quarter, or Rub Al Khali, stretched away into the distance, vast and mysterious — an impenetrable barrier to travel across the heart of the Arabian peninsula.

The challenge implicit in that apparent impenetrability, of course, was one compelling reason for the fascination the desert held for generations of adventurers. As Everest did to later explorers, the Empty Quarter stood as a silent reproach to their daring.

The challenge, of course, was more than the soft red sand and the blazing sun of popular imagination: apart from the dangers posed by hostile tribesmen, bandits, and occasionally obstructive governments, there were many different deserts to be conquered on the way across the Arabian peninsula. There were the towering sand dunes, sapping the strength of men and camels as they struggled up and down the vertiginous slopes, but there were also miles of gravel plains in the Nej'd or in the dark wastes of Abu Bahr; there were mountains and rocky outcrops, and mile upon mile of glistening, treacherous salt flats.

The travellers might start their journey climbing through the Qara Mountains of Oman, or striking inland straight into the deserts along the Gulf coast. For weeks at a time, their world would be bounded by the need to find food for their camels: in one place, grazing might be plentiful after a sudden rainfall, and elsewhere they might trek for miles without the sight of a green shoot.

For a few, there was the crippling sense of loneliness to contend with, although others said they had never felt *less* alone than they did in the desert. During the day, they would often be parched and burning from the blazing sun — but at night, they might wake shivering with cold and damp. For all of them, occasionally, there was the spectre of abject despair: the challenges to be met were psychological as well as physical.

And then, there was the race to be first: Sir Richard Burton's passion was to be the first non-Muslim to smuggle himself into the Haj caravan to Mecca, that of Wilfrid Blunt and his indomitable wife Lady Anne to be the first Europeans into the city of Hail, while in this century, Harry St John Philby and Bertram Thomas vied with each other to make the first crossing of the Rub Al Khali itself.

Along the way, there were specimens to be collected, measurements and observations to be made for the learned societies at home, and ancient ruins to be discovered and speculated on. Some, like T E Lawrence and the spies and agents of the 19th and 20th centuries, could claim military duty as the reason for their exploits; Bertram Thomas told his Arab companions that it was simply the love of travel and the pursuit of knowledge that led him into the desert.

Certainly, among many of the travellers, there was a highly-coloured and romantic view of the ancient mysteries of the Arab world tempting them on, with their lurid visions of gorgeously apparelled potentates and dusky harem beauties. They had too, all too often, a similarly self-indulgent view of themselves. Burton observed grandiloquently that a man like himself must wander or die; the Blunts described their journey as a pilgrimage undertaken in the name of romance.

The search for glittering fantasy in the grinding poverty of life among the desert Arabs was almost always certain to fail, just as much as the earlier military expeditions in search of the mythical wealth of 'Arabia Felix'. But Arabia changed the travellers: whatever they set out to find, most of them returned touched by the spirit of the desert and its people.

The peace and stillness of the sands, a natural cathedral under the black arching roof of the night sky, affected them all. "The great peace of Islam slowly and surely descended upon me," observed Philby; Burton, too, found it a holy place; Thesiger spoke movingly of the solace he had found in the hardship of desert travel.

A few were unimpressed — the misanthropic Charles Doughty, for instance, talks of the blazing torture of the desert, and compares its people with wild beasts. But even he found poor men willing to share their meagre supper with a stranger, and friends and protectors who treated him as if he were their own son. Thesiger, a century later, had no reservations: in all his travels, he said, he had found true nobility only among the bedu. "The highest standards of behaviour were the standards of the desert."

Certainly it is true that none of the travellers would have finished their journeys without the help and co-operation of their Arab companions — paid guides, who often became close friends. They, of course, made little out of their suffering — a few dollars, perhaps enough to buy a camel or a rifle — but then, so too, by and large, did the travellers themselves.

Doughty struggled to find a publisher for the great book of his travels, Burton died in poverty, and Thesiger waited nearly a decade before writing *Arabian Sands*. And yet none of them seem to have regretted their struggles under the blazing Arabian sun.

Merchants, Pilgrims and Invaders

"Here are people that sift the pure fine gold of Arabia Felix…
the Arabs that ever shift their dwellings…"

– Miguel de Cervantes, *Don Quixote*

The Empty Quarter itself may have defied travellers, but around its fringes lay a whole network of ancient routes. Merchants' caravans travelled laboriously up the Red Sea coast, carrying the white dusty tear-drops of frankincense from Yemen and Oman north to Petra, and on to Damascus, Cairo, and the West, where priests burned it as incense, and doctors administered it as a cure for a whole range of ailments. It was even offered as an antidote to the poison hemlock, and, although modern physicians regard it as wholly valueless, an entire economy was built upon the milk-like juice which seeped from the cut branches of the frankincense trees, hardening as it came into contact with the air.

Today, the trade barely survives, as Wilfred Thesiger's description of a meeting with a twentieth century version of the trading caravan demonstrates: two men, with four camels tied head to tail. That, he said, was what the ancient trade had come to — hardly more important to the people of southern Arabia than the market in goats and firewood.

But centuries ago, well-worn trails twisted up the eastern side of the peninsula for caravans laden not only with frankincense, but also with silks, spices, gold, precious stones, ivory, rare woods, and other merchandise that had been brought from Africa, India, and even China by the Arab merchant fleets. Trade kept alive a succession of South Arabian civilisations for 1,500 years or more, and the caravans were carefully regulated, with government officials levying tolls and customs dues as they passed through the various states. There are accounts of a massive building programme in the Hadramaut, where masonry walls sealed off wadis to force travellers to pass through the great gate of Qalat, for their cargoes to be assessed and taxed. The gate was set in a fifteen-foot stone wall which was some six hundred feet long, and led to a closely-guarded pass between the mountainside and the wadi. Such was the degree of organisation of the spice routes, and merchants tried to circumvent it at their peril. The Roman historian Pliny describes how the kings of Shabwa, in the Hadramaut, would have any travellers who dared to leave the official road summarily executed.

It was not until the fourth or fifth centuries AD that the importance of the desert trails began to diminish. Ships were travelling the Red Sea and the Indian Ocean with more confidence, and traders had begun to bypass the middlemen of Southern Arabia. During the years of plenty, the people of what is now Yemen had constructed a massive dam at Marib — and, as trade and prosperity gradually ebbed away, so the dam sank into disrepair. Its final catastrophic collapse in the late sixth century marks the end of a millennium and a half of affluence for the whole region. The great agricultural gardens it had watered dried up and returned to the desert, and the ancient trading routes were slowly forgotten.

As the caravans had wound their way northwards, travellers' tales began to spread of the mystical and fabulously wealthy land from which they had come. Winged serpents guarded the frankincense trees, declared Herodotus in the fifth century BC, while four hundred years later, Diodorus Siculus was writing that the gold mines of Arabia were so pure that there was no need to smelt the metal that was dug from the ground.

The shrewd merchants, of course, would have been unwilling to reveal exactly where their rich cargoes came from, even if they knew; what could be more natural then, than that the people in the souqs or markets at the northern end of the spice routes should assume that all the merchandise originated in Southern Arabia itself. It was, it seemed, truly 'Arabia Felix' — a land of boundless wealth.

Very occasionally, stories like that would tempt foreign armies, emboldened by military vainglory and the courage of past conquests, to march into the desert from the north. The Romans came in the year 24 BC at the order of the Emperor Augustus, with Aelius Gallus marching for nine hundred miles at the head of the Legions. He hoped to push the power of Imperial Rome into the Arabian peninsula, and to win for the Emperor control of the riches of the merchants' caravans. Gallus, proconsul of Egypt, forced Syllaeus, one of the leading citizens of the nominally independent city of Petra, to guide his forces south. In high hopes, the troops sailed down the Red Sea in a fleet of ships, and started the long march towards the Hadramaut.

It was a disaster, and Gallus turned on his guide, not believing that any country in the world could be as cruel as this. Surely, he said, Syllaeus had deliberately led the army through the most arid and desolate lands he could find! The truth of it is that Syllaeus probably had no need of such treachery. For an ill-prepared army, not expecting the blistering heat of the desert trail, the usual routes of southern Arabia would have been all but impassable.

Gallus never reached the cities of the south: instead, he led back a bedraggled and disheartened rabble, which claimed to have won victories over huge numbers of raiding tribesmen, but had been defeated by the desert sun and their lack of knowledge of the country.

The historian Strabo, writing some thirty years later, set out the epitaph of the general's disaster: "The men who were lost were lost not by war, but because of hunger, sickness, fatigue, lack of water, and bad roads," he wrote, summing up the harsh reality that travellers were to find in peace and in war for generations to follow.

It was many centuries before the hard lesson the Romans had learned was forgotten, but in the twelfth century, the Crusader Renaud de Chatillon led an army of marauding adventurers and desperados down the desert route, in high hopes of winning booty by sacking the city of Medina. The Arab armies waited until the intruders, weakened by their long trek through blazing heat, were only a day's march from the city, and then fell on them mercilessly. Those who had endured the journey died in the battle, and the few who survived that were taken to Mecca and stoned to death as infidels and invaders.

But even for those who came in peace, the Arabian desert was a cruel adversary. In the centuries that followed the life of the Prophet Mohammed (Peace Be Upon Him), the annual Haj pilgrim caravans struggled each year through the blazing heat towards the holy cities of Mecca and Medina. The biggest of the caravans started from Damascus, to be joined on its way by other groups of pilgrims coming from central Asia, Russia and Kurdistan on a terrifying journey across the great deserts of Syria and northern Arabia. Travellers described with wonder the way that preparations for the journey took over the city — the souqs full of strangers and foreigners, bargaining fiercely as they stocked up with essentials for the trek; the caravan drivers urging their huge shuffling camels through the narrow streets; the serving men busily stuffing pillows under the pack saddle frames to protect the great beasts from sores on their four-month journey.

Many of the pilgrims brought goods from their own countries to sell in the souq, hoping to meet some of the costs of the pilgrimage — carpets, silks, and shawls from Turkey, European shoes, hardware and trinkets, and snakes and leather goods from Yemen. Often, of course, they were disappointed: the shrewd merchants of Damascus would have known how desperate they were to sell, and the prices they offered would have been correspondingly meagre.

But no hardship could halt the determined pilgrims, and the sheer scale of the nineteenth-century Haj as it left the city is described by the

English traveller Charles Doughty. "The length of the slow-footed multitudes of men and cattle is near two miles, and the width some hundred yards in the open plains. The hajjaj were this year by their own account some 6,000 persons — of these more than half are serving men on foot —and 10,000 of all kinds of cattle."

Camels, mules, asses and dromedaries all accompanied the great march as it wound its way slowly southwards towards Arabia, the great snow-covered Mount Hermon behind them. Each day, a lightly-loaded group of servants would press on ahead of the main body of pilgrims, pitching camp ready for them at a pre-arranged spot. At night, said Doughty, the military tents of the escorting soldiers were pitched sixty yards or so apart, around the mass of the pilgrims, with paper lanterns hanging outside them until dawn — or until the poorly-paid soldiers, anxious to sell as many of their candles as they could, had blown them out at night.

"They suffer none to pass their lines unchallenged. Great is all townsmen's dread of the bedu, as if they were the demons of this wild waste earth, ever ready to assail the Haj passengers," he wrote. By five-thirty in the morning, the pilgrims were out of their tents and on their way again, following the Derb-el-Haj, a track that generations of caravans had trampled into the gravel and clay of the barren upland wastes.

Other caravans, witness to the overwhelming spread of Islam, journeyed from Cairo, and Baghdad, and still more from closer destinations such as Riyadh, Hail, Muscat, and Yemen — Moors, Turks, Persians, Indians, Chinese, Africans, and Malays, all converging year after year on the holy shrines of Mecca. The English poet Wilfrid Scawen Blunt and his wife joined the Persian caravan on its way back from the Haj. "The procession, three miles long, was composed of some four thousand camels," wrote Lady Anne. "In front were the dervishes, walking very fast, almost running — wild, dirty people, but amiable, and quite ready to converse if they knew Arabic; then a group of respectably dressed people, walking out of piety... Some way behind these forerunners comes the *berak*, or banner, carried in the centre of a group of mounted dromedaries magnificently caparisoned and moving on at a fast walk... and after the berak comes the mass of pilgrims, mounted sometimes two on one camel, sometimes with a couple of boxes on each side, the household furniture..."

The better class of pilgrims — and of course, all the women — travelled in *mahmals* or litters on the back of a camel, covered with blue or red canvas, while one or two of the wealthy were in larger carriages carried by two beasts, one before and one behind. But it was no easy journey, even for them. Later, the Blunts described the arrival of the pilgrims at the town of Nejef, in Iraq. "Many of the camels had rushed into the lake to drink, and lain down there never to get up again. Others could just move one foot before the other, following at a rate of perhaps a mile an hour, with hopeless glazed eyes and poor emaciated bodies..." There had been, they said, delays and mismanagement on the return journey, although this time at least, all the pilgrims in the train survived the journey.

Only the extremely wealthy could afford to travel independently of the main body of the Haj, and in a certain amount of luxury. The Arabic historian Taki el Fasi, for instance, describes how Suleiman ibn Abd El Malik journeyed in the seventh century with nine hundred camels bearing his wardrobe alone; and six centuries later, Nasir Eddyn Abou el Maly, Sultan of Egypt, outdid even that splendour. The Sultan included with his personal train five hundred camels to carry his sweetmeats and confectionery, and another two hundred and eighty laden with pomegranates, almonds, and fruit, and — presumably to enable him to enjoy a balanced diet — one thousand geese and three thousand fowls were taken along as well.

Those, of course, are the glittering stories beloved by historians, but for the great crowd of the pilgrims, the Haj must have been a long and terrible struggle. Millions of them made the journey, from all over the Muslim world, making the Arabian peninsula one of the most cosmopolitan international crossroads and routeways of the medieval world. It was a mass movement of people which carried its own dangers with it, over and above the hardships and hazards of the desert crossing itself. In 1865, for instance, the plague ran through the caravan as it returned from the pilgrimage, sweeping through Egypt and leaving more than fifty thousand people dead in its wake.

Sometimes non-Muslims would join the caravan in disguise, driven by either curiosity or a spirit of adventure, although they risked death if they were discovered in the region of the holy cities. In the 1850s, Richard Burton joined the Haj in Medina, disguised as an Arab sheikh. By coming so late to the pilgrimage, he had missed much of the suffering of the journey, but he still described the panic which hit the caravan as a band of robbers staged an ambush, and his own frustration as they marched patiently on through the night. "I can hardly find words to express the weary horrors of the long, dark march, during which the hapless traveller, fuming... with disappointment in his hopes of seeing the country, is compelled to sit upon the back of a creeping camel," he wrote bitterly.

But, despite the lost hours of darkness, he still managed to set down his own impressions of a rich but inhospitable landscape. "Nowhere had I seen a land in which the earth's anatomy lies so barren, or one richer in volcanic or primary formations," he said.

Doughty's journey with the pilgrims came twenty years or so later. His aim was to reach the ancient sites of Medain Salih in Saudi Arabia, although his journey marked the start of an extraordinary series of wanderings described in detail in a later chapter. He travelled in the disguise of a Persian, his beard dyed with henna — a solitary non-Muslim among the thousands of devout pilgrims. Some of his loneliness comes out in his description of the journey. "All charity is cold in the great and terrible wilderness of that wayworn, suffering multitude," he wrote. "The lonely, indigent man, without succour, who falls in the empty wilderness, is desolate indeed. When the great convoy is passed from him, and he is forsaken of all mankind, if any bedu find him fainting, it is but likely that they will strip him... None upon the road will do a gentle deed but for silver."

Part of that bitterness, no doubt, is a result of the man's own deception: neither Doughty nor Burton, outsiders travelling alone and secretly among a crowd of enthusiastic pilgrims, could have expected to share a sense of religious fellow-feeling and togetherness.

But the hardships were real: neither of the two impostors made the whole journey of the Haj, and there is no doubting the suffering that the pilgrims themselves must have endured on the rest of the route, and on the homeward trail as well.

For all the dangers and difficulties, the pilgrims were travelling a known and charted route. Like the soldiers and traders who had made their way through Arabia before them, they knew there were supplies of water, scanty and brackish though they might be, on the road ahead. Fortified *kellas* or water stations, protected by iron-plated doors and garrisons of soldiers, dotted the route at long and irregular intervals. Although it might have been two or three days' march from one to another, at least the water supplies were known and plans made accordingly.

All the travellers kept to the side of the great wastes of the Empty Quarter. Travelling into the sands, they were well aware, would mean death just as certainly as swimming out into the ocean. There was no hope of survival, nothing to sustain life — and, just as important, no reason to make the journey. The Empty Quarter, they all knew, was just that — empty, barren, and hostile. It was best left alone.

SPIES AND STORYTELLERS

"One of the gladdest moments in human life is the departure
upon a distant journey into unknown lands"

– Sir Richard Burton

For centuries, it was the illicit and dangerous trip to Mecca and the Holy Shrines which was the magnet drawing European adventurers, vagabonds, and travellers into the Arabian peninsula. The desert was no more than an obstacle to be overcome, albeit a terrifying and romantic one which, according to the characters of the explorers, might even add to the appeal of the journey.

Many travelled in disguise, taking advantage of the cosmopolitan nature of the Haj or the trading caravans to masquerade as Muslims from Afghanistan, India, or central Asia, while others went as slaves, bought and sold in the markets of the Ottoman Empire. They have left behind few memories of their journeys: the self-styled Gentleman of Rome, Ludovico di Varthema, wrote in the early sixteenth century of the ceaseless swaying of the camels as the caravan made its way across the desert towards Medina, of the pilgrims dying of thirst in the burning sun, and of others left to wallow and die in the treacherous quicksands along the way.

Some of his tales stretch the credibility of a literal-minded modern reader: for instance, he describes one of a pair of young unicorns which he saw at Mecca, "at the age of one year, and like a young colt; the horn of this is of the length of four handfuls..." But his descriptions of the trials and horrors of desert travel do sound like the voice of experience.

He travelled, he said, for three days and nights in "a great, broad plain, all covered with white sand, in manner as small as flour... If by evil fortune it so chance that any travel that way southward, if in the meantime the wind come to the north, they are overwhelmed with sand, that they scatter out of the way and can scarcely see one another ten paces off." He talks of travellers dying from thirst, and from over-indulging when they do eventually find water; of sun-dried bodies preserved in the dried sand, the flesh of which is considered medicinal; and of fifteen hundred desert tribesmen slaughtered in a single engagement. Travellers with experiences like that to relate may surely be forgiven the occasional unicorn!

Another, Vincent le Blanc, told sixty years later of the "fantasies and goblins" in the desert, which "strive to seduce the travellers and cause them to perish with hunger and despair", while a third, Johann Wild, described — probably more believably — one of the greatest disasters in the history of the Haj. Wild was a soldier of the Imperial Hungarian Army of the seventeenth century, who was captured by the Turks, and sold into slavery. His master took him in 1607 as a servant on the Egyptian Haj caravan — twenty thousand pilgrims and a hundred thousand camels setting out under armed escort for the eight-hundred-mile journey through the deserts to Mecca.

But many of the pilgrims never even made it as far as the Arabian peninsula: the wells on which they were relying to cross the Sinai desert were dry, and men and camels alike began to die of thirst. By the time the caravan reached Aqaba on the Red Sea, two thousand of them were dead, and more perished as they made their way across the Hejaz, attacked and harried all the way by hostile tribesmen. Perhaps it is a tribute to the Haj itself that the caravan reached Mecca at all: for Wild, sold on again as a slave and finally given his freedom, it was a minor miracle that four years later he finally reached home in Germany.

The storytellers and occasionally their motives may sometimes be suspect, but their tales are exciting, because they describe people struggling to survive in a strange and unfamiliar world. They are a reminder of how popular simple tales of adventure have been through the centuries.

But the travellers who made the journey to Mecca had little interest in the desert itself, or in the people who lived there. They took the risks of travel either because they had to, bound by law and the fear of punishment to the masters who had bought them, or because they wanted to see the forbidden holy shrines. As far as they could, they stuck to the known routes across the sands.

Until well into the nineteenth century, the Empty Quarter itself still seemed to have little appeal for explorers. In 1761, for example, the King of Denmark sponsored a great Arabian expedition, which is still seen as one of the most important episodes in the exploration of the peninsula; and yet the explorers ventured no further towards the interior to make their maps and gather their information than Sana'a in Yemen.

The Danish expedition is always linked with the name of Carsten Niebuhr — largely, no doubt, because he was the only one of the five scientists in the party to survive the malaria mosquitoes of 'Arabia Felix' and return home alive. Unlike most of their predecessors, the expedition went openly as Europeans and Christians. They were not making any secret journeys to the holy places of Islam, but instead — a doctor, a botanist, an artist, a philologist, and a surveyor — they were conducting a coherent scientific study of the region, its people, and their way of life.

A few adventurous soldiers and other travellers made forays around the edges of the Empty Quarter, apparently without the need for disguise that journeys to the Holy Cities involved. The British Navy had been patrolling the Gulf region for decades to protect the shipping routes to India; one of the officers who visited Oman, for instance, was a young midshipman named Horatio Nelson, in the year 1775. He, apparently, stayed on board his ship. But sixty years later, Lieutenant James Wellstead gazed down from the Jebel Akhdar at the Empty Quarter stretching away to the western horizon.

"Vast plains of loose drift sand, across which even the hardy Bedouin scarcely dares to venture, spread out as far as the eye could reach. Not a hill or even a change of colouring in the plains occurs to break the unvarying and desolate appearance of the scene," he wrote later, though anyone who has watched the shifting colours of a desert landscape might wonder whether the lieutenant was colour-blind.

Other soldiers made similar ventures westward from the Omani coast. Seven years after Wellsted, the Bavarian soldier of fortune Adolphe von Wrede set out from Mukalla into the Hadramaut, to be greeted by the local sheikhs as an honoured guest. Again, he looked out from the shore of the great sand-sea of the Empty Quarter. "Not a single trace of vegetation, be it so scanty, appeared to animate the vast expanse. Not a single bird interrupts with its note the calm of death." Elsewhere on his travels, the locals were less friendly, and he was beaten and chased away from one village, leaving all his belongings behind. It was a tragedy for any traveller who wanted fame and honour at home: without proof of his journey, his accounts were dismissed as lies and make-believe.

One military traveller who had gone further than anyone else without disguise was Captain George Sadlier, of His Majesty's 47th Foot, who was despatched from India in 1819 to convey His Majesty's congratulations to the victorious Egyptian armies in Arabia, and set about his mission with a will. Unfortunately, he couldn't find the Egyptian commander, Ibrahim. He landed at Hasa, to find the Egyptians had moved on, and so he travelled east with their rearguard to Manfuhuh, near Riyadh.

The attitude of the lightly-armed and desert-hardened Egyptian troops to the sweating English officer they were expected to escort can be imagined. At Manfuhuh, he found Ibrahim had moved on to Diriyyah; at Diriyyah, he had gone on to Rass; at Rass, he had left for Medina. By the time he caught up with the Egyptian command, he was thoroughly sick of the entire mission — even more so when he was told at Medina that it was not possible for him to enter the town, and that he must make his camp with the women.

When he finally saw Ibrahim, he was again disappointed. The Egyptian commander greeted him affably enough, although he was clearly bemused by both message and messenger. But he had no interest in Sadlier's other proposal, an alliance against the coastal tribes of the Gulf, and he had him packed straight off with the women to the port of Yanbu. The indignity was immense, but Sadlier's achievement, whether he wanted it or not, was considerable. Bundled around like an item of luggage as he was, he had still crossed the continent from one side to another. And, even more impressive, he had done it openly, without disguise.

But the time for openness had not come yet. The Hejaz was in torment, with the Egyptian forces of the Ottoman Empire mounting campaign after campaign against the determined Wahhabi tribesmen of the interior. The Egyptian troops, incidentally, brought with them a sprinkling of European soldiers, men who had either been captured and converted to Islam to save their lives, or wanderers who had joined the Ottoman forces for their own reasons. One of them, the Scottish drummer boy Thomas Keith, enjoyed the unlikely distinction of being appointed Governor of Medina.

For most foreigners, though, the tumult made Arabia an even more dangerous place in which to travel; even for those, like Johann Ludwig Burckhardt, who were not actively serving foreign governments as spies and secret agents. Burckhardt, a Swiss adventurer, travelled under the sponsorship of the grandly-titled Association for Promoting the Discovery of the Interior Parts of Africa, an organisation which seems to have taken a slightly relaxed view of its own terms of reference. His travels in Arabia, by his own account, were simply a preparation for a journey of exploration to Timbuktu, although he pursued them with a zeal which suggests they had an attraction of their own. Before he even arrived in the Arabian peninsula, nervously explaining the grotesque foreign accent of his Arabic with a pretence that Hindustani was his mother-tongue, he had already become the first European to visit the ruined city of Petra. Once a major destination of the traditional Arabian trading routes, Petra had been forgotten for centuries by the outside world, but Burckhardt was not satisfied by his discovery. Instead, he travelled on to Cairo, and from there into Arabia itself.

Burckhardt claimed that his pilgrimage to Mecca, dressed as a poor traveller and still taking refuge in a pretended Hindustani background, was intended to improve his standing in the Islamic world, and thus improve his chances of reaching Timbuktu, but by now he was clearly seized by the fascination with Arabia which seems to have gripped many of the travellers who came to the desert. He spent more than two years wandering through Arabia disguised as Sheikh Ibrahim, while the war between Egyptians and Wahhabis raged around him. At one point, he was set upon by dogs from a bedu encampment, adding with wounded dignity, "I had much difficulty, though mounted, to defend myself from their teeth". Later, he describes how he walked ahead of the caravan during the night, only to find that it failed to catch up with him. "I retraced my steps," he says, "and found the camels standing at rest and taking breath, and every soul upon them fast asleep... When the camel hears no voices about it, and is not urged by the leader, it slackens its pace, and at last stands still to rest; and if the leading camel once stops, all the others do the same."

But Burckhardt's interest lay more with the towns and their people than with the deserts and the tribes of the interior. His travels took him more than two years, and left him with his health shattered by the plague, and he never made the journey into Africa for which his whole life had supposedly been a preparation. He died in Egypt at the age of 31, a victim of the plague.

Although Burckhardt travelled in disguise, there is no evidence that he was anything more than a traveller or a scientific observer. He never converted to Islam, but his respect for the religion of the Arab world was genuine: he was buried in Cairo under the Muslim name he had taken for his travels, Pilgrim Ibrahim ibn Abdallah.

But nationalism and religious fervour were sweeping the Arabian peninsula, ripping apart the remnants of the Ottoman administration, and the nineteenth century saw the growth of another class of travellers in Arabia, the spies and agents of foreign governments, slipping secretly through the country to gather information about the complex politics of the region. Russia, France, Britain, and Egypt all had their own interests in the peninsula, and all, for their own reasons, wanted to know about the strength of the new, strictly religious Wahhabi movement which, by the early nineteenth century, had seized control of Mecca and much of the interior of Arabia.

Again, the stories of these mysterious figures are compelling in their own right: the French spy Badia-y-Leblich, for instance, travelled from Morocco to Cairo and on into Arabia, journeying around Mecca and Jeddah in the guise of an Abbasid prince, while at the same time, Ulrich Jasper Seetzen was starting on the same secret journey on behalf of Czar Alexander I of Russia, dressed sometimes as a beggar and sometimes as an Arab physician. Forty years later, George Augustus Wallin struggled across the Nafud Desert in the service of the Egyptians, sending back intelligence about the city of Hail and its territory — the same mysterious city that Wilfrid Blunt and his wife were to visit another forty years later.

Often, it seems that the Arab authorities in the various towns through which they passed saw through their disguises — Wallin pretended to be a travelling horse-dealer — but for their own reasons allowed them to continue. If the European powers were interested in Arabia, the Arabs were often interested in playing off the Europeans against each other.

At least, for a time: some of the spies escaped from Arabia — Wallin, for instance, ended his life as Helsinki's Professor of Oriental Languages — but others were less lucky. Malaria or other diseases accounted for many; others were executed or quietly done away with. Seetzen, the German who was spying for the Russian Czar, died mysteriously in Yemen, either from sickness or from poison.

And yet, if these men were not simply explorers, they were not only spies either. For some, the sponsorship of some foreign power offered the only realistic chance of travelling through Arabia. Many of them were fascinated by the desert and the Arab way of life.

A few years after Wallin, a French spy followed a similar route — William Gifford Palgrave, a son of one of England's most respected families. His brother Francis, as Professor of Poetry at Oxford University, compiled the classic *Palgrave's Golden Treasury*, another brother edited *The Economist*, and a third became Clerk of the House of Commons. William Gifford Palgrave, though, had always been a rebel. He insisted on joining the Indian Army rather than following the career mapped out for him as a churchman and an academic, and ten years later, impressed by the commitment of Napoleon III to the defence of Christians in Lebanon, he became a secret agent of the French government.

His journey in 1862, like Wallin's, took him across the red Nafud Desert at the heart of Arabia. "It proved worse than aught imagined," he wrote later, "...an immense ocean of loose reddish sand, heaped up in enormous ridges running parallel to each other from north to south... In the depths between, the traveller finds himself imprisoned as it were in a suffocating sand pit, hemmed in by burning walls on every side." It was the height of summer — the very worst time of year to attempt a desert crossing — but Palgrave and his party struggled on through a landscape which he said reminded him of nothing so much as Dante's Inferno, until eventually they reached the oasis city of Hail. From there, they travelled on into the heartland of Arabia, to Diriyyah, the birthplace of the Wahhabi movement, but now a ruin, sacked by the Egyptian army more than forty years before, and from there to the nearby city of Riyadh.

In Riyadh Palgrave describes how he maintained his disguise as an Arab doctor by administering medicine to the people, and how the various factions in the palace tried to involve him in their intrigues. It was too dangerous a place to stay, and the party slipped away secretly to head for the Gulf coast.

As they struggled across the Dahna Desert on their way to Hofuf, they came across a swarm of locusts. "It was a thorough godsend to our Arabs, on no account to be neglected," wrote Palgrave. "Thirst, weariness, all was forgotten, and down the riders leapt from their sad, staring camels: this one spread out a cloak, that a saddlebag, a third his shirt, over the unlucky creatures destined for the morrow's meal."

Hungry as he was, Palgrave couldn't bring himself to try the delicacy. The excited Arabs were left to capture as many of the tasty morsels as they could, while he and his friends pressed on to Hofuf, where he sat down to his first meal of fresh fish for six months. The fish, apparently, was more appetising than the locusts.

He spent several more months travelling around the Gulf, in Qatar, Oman, and Persia, before returning to Britain. How successful his mission had been in terms of the intelligence he had sent back to his masters in Paris is, in the nature of things, hardly likely to be known, but he had completed the first diagonal crossing of the Arabian peninsula by a European, and on the way, had been the first to visit both the hidden cities of Hail and Riyadh.

Victorian England, still supremely confident of its mission to rule the world, had an insatiable appetite for tales of bravery and derring-do by its own young heroes in exotic lands. Palgrave's *Personal Narrative of a Year's Journey Through Central and Eastern Arabia*, written up by him in a German monastery in the months after his return, was a runaway success. It was not the first book of its kind, though: ten years earlier, a very different author had described his own journeyings in Arabia. Sir Richard Burton was in many ways the most complex and most interesting of the adventurers who made their way in disguise to the Muslim Holy Cities; neither a spy nor really an explorer, but rather a traveller and adventurer for whom the journey was its own justification.

Burton, with all the faults of his time, affected to despise every race but his own, and yet studied their languages and customs with a passion and a determination to understand. By the time he died, he was fluent in forty-one different languages, from Persian, Gujarati, and Arabic to Swahili and the sign-language of the American Indians — although he never considered himself proficient in a language until he could be taken for a native when he spoke it. He studied and discussed the religions of the different countries in which he travelled with care: he learned some fifty thousand words of the Holy Qura'n, and after his travels in Arabia, he adopted the pilgrim's habit of carrying his own shroud in his baggage. It does not sound like a description of the racist bully so often associated with the name of Sir Richard Burton.

But why did Burton and the others choose to take such risks to travel through Arabia, a country about which they must have had only the haziest and most inaccurate of ideas? Burton put it down to his character as 'a thoroughbred wanderer'. For a man like himself, he declared grandly, the excitement of travel is the only cure for "a paroxysm of ennui... he walks about his room all night, he yawns at conversations, and a book acts upon him as a narcotic. The man wants to wander, and he must do so, or he shall die."

To win the support and sponsorship of the Royal Geographical Society, he set out an earnest list of objectives: to investigate the possibility of setting up a Central Arabian stud market to supply British India with horses; to obtain information on the Empty Quarter itself; to study the water-supplies of the Hejaz; and to investigate the racial origins of the Arab peoples. To accomplish that daunting programme, he proposed a trip to take him diagonally across Arabia, through Medina or Mecca to Muscat and the Indian Ocean.

He was not a government spy; the value the British government put on his services can be seen by the Foreign Office post they offered him a few years later, as consul of Fernando Po, a disease-ridden little island some twenty miles off the west coast of Africa. His real ambitions were personal rather than political.

By the standards he had announced, his journey was a failure; he accomplished practically none of his objectives. But, like most of the spies and eccentrics who preceded him and followed him, Burton had an ulterior motive of his own. He wanted to visit the forbidden cities of Islam.

Burton's character suggests that he would have wanted to travel there in any case, simply because they were forbidden, but he was also a man fascinated by people and religions. He admitted later that his main emotion as he stood in the centre of Mecca and gazed upon the sacred Kaaba was one of pride in his own achievement, but he also said: "I may truly say that, of all the worshippers who clung weeping to the curtain, or who pressed their beating hearts to the stone, none felt for the moment a deeper emotion than did the Haji from the far north. It was as if the poetical legends of the Arabs spoke truth, and that the waving wings of angels, not the sweet breeze of morning, were agitating and swelling the black covering of the shrine."

In some ways, Burton had an easier journey than some of the other explorers. He avoided much of the long trek through the desert, as did many of the pilgrims, by taking a boat as far as the Red Sea port of Yanbu, only joining the Damascus caravan at Medina. The sea-crossing, of course, had difficulties and dangers of its own — including several fist-fights among the travellers which Burton seems to relish as much in the telling as in the actuality — but it was an easier journey than the terrible slog along the Haj route.

On the journey that he did make through the desert, from Yanbu to Medina and then on to Mecca, the young subaltern rented a litter, or *shugduf*, for himself, so that he could travel in relative comfort, slung between two camels. He had injured a foot by stepping on a sea-urchin as he came ashore at Yanbu, but the great advantage of the litter was that it would allow him to take notes and make sketches without fear of discovery. Even so, he was cautious enough to cut his drawings into tiny squares, which he meticulously numbered before hiding them away in his medicine chest. The precautions against discovery were necessary, but Burton's book gives the clear impression that he thoroughly enjoyed the secrecy and intrigue for its own sake.

Litter or not, the journey included all the dangers and discomforts that his predecessors had faced: attacks and ambushes by tribesmen, thirst, and weariness. And always, there was the unforgiving, harsh terrain: "On either side were ribbed precipices, dark, angry, and towering above, till their summits mingled with the gloom of night; and between them, formidable looked the chasm down which our host hurried with shouts and discharges of matchlocks," he wrote. "There was no path. Rocks, stone banks, and trees obstructed our passage. The camels, now blind with darkness, then dazzled by a flood of light, stumbled frequently, in some places slipping down a steep descent, in others sliding over a sheet of mud." One suspects that Burton was not going to minimise the dangers and difficulties in his writings about his travels.

But the main interest of his account is his description of the effect of the desert landscape upon himself. None of the other travellers through Arabia have matched him, a man of all faiths and of none as he was, for his account of the mystical, almost religious effect of the silence of the desert. Perhaps it was the solitude within the crowd which his deception forced on him, but the boorish, roustabout Burton seems occasionally to have found the sands a still, silent cathedral.

"It was a desert peopled only with echoes — a place of death for what little there is to die in it — a wilderness where, to use my companion's phrase, there is nothing but He," he wrote, adding, in a pedantic little footnote: "*La siwa hu* — ie, where there is none but Allah".

After completing his pilgrimage, Burton's ideas of continuing his planned route across central Arabia to Muscat seem to have evaporated. "Worn out with fatigue and the fatal fiery heat," he says, he hurried to Jeddah to take a ship for Suez. Still in Arab dress, he was accosted by an English officer, who kicked him and shouted: "Get out of the way, you dirty nigger!" — a remark which seems more of a tribute to Burton's disguise than to the standards of behaviour of the British Empire.

Unwelcome Stranger

*"How desperate a thing it were, to be abandoned in the midst
of the wilderness of Arabia; where we dread to meet with
unknown mankind more than with wild beasts!"*

– Charles Doughty

The question Charles Doughty was repeatedly asked by the puzzled Arabs with whom he stayed and travelled during his two years of wandering through Arabia was a simple one: "Why did you come?" He never gave an answer to the Arabs, and he never gives an answer to the readers of his books. He misses few chances to denigrate either the people he was travelling among, or the country itself, and much of his journeying seems to have been undertaken in hopes of getting away from Arabia once and for all.

His initial journey with the Haj to the relics of Medain Salih, on the road to Mecca and Medina, was adventurous enough, but it had at least a clearly defined objective, following on from Burckhardt's rediscovery of Petra sixty-four years earlier. For a man like Doughty, who had already been travelling for several years like some Victorian hippy scholar from place to place through Europe, the fascination of another ruined Nabataean city was immense. He wanted to be the first European to see and record the ancient inscriptions, much as Burckhardt had described the carvings and buildings of Petra. That involved balancing precariously on the end of a wooden beam propped against the crumbling walls as he prepared impressions of the inscriptions onto soaking blotting paper, which he allowed to dry in the sun. It was three months before he had completed most of his task.

He had been posted with five rough soldiers of the Ottoman Empire who garrisoned the little fort or *kella* near Medain Salih, and he spent an uncomfortable and occasionally dangerous time with them, bullied, threatened, and almost murdered by their commander, Mohammed Ali — "a fiend dim with the leprosy of the soul, and half-fond," as he described him later.

He seems to have had little regard for the Arabs or, as a ferocious religious bigot, for their religion, and his provocative manner must have often incited his companions to violence; but something in that three months must have sparked his imagination, because he let the returning Haj caravan travel on without him.

The pilgrims and the soldiers alike — even the savage Mohammed Ali — begged him to stay with the caravan. "Think better for thyself," the pilgrims urged him, "and return with us while the way is open, from this hunger-stricken wilderness consumed by the sun; thou wast not bred, and God calls thee not, to this suffering in a land which only demons can inhabit."

Their words must have come back to him again and again in the following months, but he would not listen. Instead, he rode off with Zeyd, his bedu guide around the ruins — "a swarthy, nearly black sheikh of the desert, of mid stature and middle age, with a hunger-bitten stern visage". Doughty had probably no idea of how long his travelling would last, but he was committed to living the life of a nomadic Arab.

Even after the time he had already spent in the desert, the intensity of the heat as he rode away with Zeyd's *tarqiy*, or band of companions, seems to have taken him unawares. "The sun stands up as a crown of hostile flames from the huge covert of inhospitable sandstone bergs. Entering as a tyrant upon the waste landscape, it darts upon us a torrent of fiery beams. Grave is that giddy heat upon the crown of the head: the ears tingle with a flickering shrillness... the hot sand-blink is in the eyes, and there is little refreshment to find in the tents' shelter. The worsted booths leak to the rain of sunny light.

"Mountains looming like dry bones through the thin air stand far round about us," he wrote.

Often, he says, he would lie awake at night, tortured by thirst, because he could not bring himself to sip the brackish, discoloured water that was drawn from the desert wells.

All the desert explorers — and, indeed, all the bedu themselves — must have felt such hardships. But, while most of the Europeans who travelled through the desert did so with paid guides and companions, Doughty threw in his lot with poor travelling nomads, offering them nothing in return but his scanty supplies of eyewashes and medicines, and his equally sketchy medical knowledge. He relied greatly upon the traditions of hospitality, although he seldom seems to have shown much gratitude — but the result is that he comes closest to describing the back-breaking, grinding harshness of everyday life for the bedu tribesmen. Where other travellers, either amused or horrified, watched their companions scramble for locusts as a welcome titbit on a long journey, Doughty watched the women of the Fukara tribe frying the insects and grinding them down to a powder which, eaten with sour buttermilk, might stave off the worst attacks of hunger.

He saw their illness: Bilharzia from polluted water, ophthalmia and other eye diseases from the searing desert sun, rheumatics, intestinal infections, and even the dreaded smallpox. At one point, he was shown the pit in the desert, a yard deep, in which a fire would be lit and a smallpox victim seated among the embers in an attempt to sweat out the disease. The settlements were no healthier than the hard life of the desert: "Who is infirm at Kheybar, he is likely to die", Doughty observed gloomily, while he was staying later in that town. But he also saw the generosity with which, with occasional exceptions, they would share what little they had with their companions or with a passing traveller.

Doughty travelled with the Fukara for three months, going with them into the town of Teyma, where he offered cures for the townsfolks' ailments and fought off, with better or worse grace, their good-humoured attempts to persuade him to embrace Islam and stay with them. By this time, though, the tribe's patience with their guest was wearing thin. Doughty had started quarrelling with Zeyd — hardly surprisingly, as both his host and his young wife would call the stranger in aid during their frequent quarrels and arguments — and he decided to set off eastwards for Hail, where the Emir, Mohammed ibn Rashid, maintained his summer palace.

Once again, Doughty was ignoring the advice of his companions: he had already experienced a degree of hostility as a Christian, or Nasrani, and further east, he was told, he would be in constant danger. It was suggested several times that ibn Rashid, who had been warned of the Englishman wandering through the country, might simply have his head cut off. In fact, though, the weary traveller was greeted courteously at the court, despite an unfortunate incident when the Emir asked him to demonstrate his skill at reading Arabic. Invited to read at random from an Arab history book, he chose a passage which translated "The king slew all his brethren and kindred" — not a tactful choice to read to a man who had indeed waded to his position through the blood of his own murdered relatives.

Despite that regrettable lapse of taste, he was kindly enough received — ibn Rashid was probably treating Doughty cautiously, as a man who might have powerful friends among the authorities of the Ottoman Empire — and provided with food and lodging. Members of the Emir's own family even came to him for medicines, including ibn Rashid's son and heir Hamud, who asked diffidently and unsuccessfully if Doughty had a cure for impotence. The traveller's other potions, however, seem to have been more effective, although Doughty wrote later that in nearly two years' travelling, he earned less than ten riyals through his medicine.

He stayed in Hail for some three weeks, and was only persuaded to leave by the obvious impatience of his hosts to see the back of him. "I asked, as the Emir was going, 'When shall I depart?' — 'At thy pleasure' — 'Tomorrow?' — 'Nay, today'." It could hardly have been a clearer hint.

By the time he finally rode out on the way to Kheybar, he had been pushed and jostled by the palace slaves, beaten in the street, and had some of his possessions stolen. Apparently in one of his frequent fits of pique, he refused the offer of dates, flour and buttermilk as supplies for the journey: but, on the other hand, he was carrying with him a safe conduct pass signed by the Emir himself.

It was indeed time to leave. The bedu who had been paid by the Emir to escort him towards Kheybar warned him as they mounted their camels: "Make haste along with us out of Hail, stand not, nor return upon thy footsteps, for then they will kill thee...!"

It was a long, hard journey to Kheybar. Doughty was forced to walk while his companions rode the camels. Several times, he was threatened with death, and only saved by the warning that he was under ibn Rashid's protection. Eventually, his companions abandoned him at a small camp in the desert, where a couple of families were herding sheep and goats. As was to happen again and again on his travels, Doughty was to be saved by the open-handedness of his poverty-stricken hosts. "As we sat about the evening fire, he brought me in a bowl of their evening milk, made hot; 'We have nothing,' he said, 'here to eat, no dates, no rice, no bread, but drink this which the Lord provideth, though it be a poor supper.' I blessed him, and said it was the best of all nourishment..." When the camel herder was told how Doughty's companions had deserted him, he declared that he would have cut their heads off had he known about it, because of their breaking of their trust. As Doughty's companions, or *rafiks*, they were bound by their honour to protect him and accompany him to the destination that had been agreed.

From this desert camp, he travelled with another bedu *rafik* named Ghroceyb the four-day journey on to Kheybar, passing through the volcanic mountains which form some of the highest parts of the

Arabian peninsula, at some six thousand feet. "The volcanic field is a stony flood which has stiffened — long rolling heads, like horse manes of those slaggy waves, ride and over-ride the rest: and as they are risen, they stand petrified, many being sharply split lengthwise, and the hollow laps are partly fallen down in vast shells and in ruinous heaps as of massy masonry," he wrote. Elsewhere, golden-red pillars of rock stood up above the black lava, "sandstone spires touched by the scattered beams of the morning sun", and away on the horizon, the travellers could see the tantalising glisten of distant water — which turned out to be no more than dry, baked clay, glazed over with salt.

Doughty had paid Ghroceyb four riyals to take him to Kheybar, but as they grew closer to the town, where the Ottoman authorities were based, the Arab grew more and more nervous. He had wanted the money to settle a blood debt which had arisen out of his killing of a man, and he was worried that the authorities might seize him when he arrived in the town. But Ghroceyb stuck to his bargain, and delivered his companion in through the gates of Kheybar to the house of a man he knew; he himself slipped away early the next morning, before anyone could recognise him.

From Doughty's description, Kheybar seems to have offered a glimpse of hell, with its sulphurous water, and its black volcanic sand. In the burial ground, he said, "the funeral earth is chapped and ghastly, bulging over her enwombed corpses like a garden soil in spring time which is pushed by the new-spiring plants. All is horror at Kheybar! — nothing there which does not fill a stranger's eye with discomfort."

Later in his journeying, Doughty observed that he was generally better treated by the wandering bedu than by people of the towns and villages. "How pleasant is the easy humour of all bedouins, in comparison with the harsher temper of townsfolk," he wrote. Certainly his stay in Kheybar seems to bear that out. Several times, only the Dowla, Abdullah, representative of Ottoman authority, saved his life from the angry townspeople who would gladly have beaten or stoned him to death, but Doughty felt no gratitude towards him. "Slavespirited", he called him, and the longer he stayed in Kheybar, the more he resented his authority.

But he did find one friend in the town: Mohammed en-Nejumy, who offered him hospitality and, according to Doughty, "became to me as a father at Kheybar". It must have been an odd relationship; the crusty Englishman repeatedly offended his host with his outspoken contempt for the Arab world, while Mohammed found Doughty's arrogance almost beyond belief. He also found at least as much to wonder at in Doughty's descriptions of England as Doughty had found in Arabia. One day, for instance, he found the drowned body of a fox in his well. Doughty "told the good man how, for a fox-brush, sheikhs in my beled used to ride furiously, in red mantles, upon horses — the best of them worth the rent of some village — with an hundred yelling curs scouring before them; and leaping over walls and dykes, they put their necks and all in adventure... For a moment, the subtle Arabian regarded me with his piercing eyes as if he would say 'Makest thou mirth of me...?'"

Perhaps one reason for Mohammed's forbearance towards him was the conviction that his guest was not only mad himself, but came from a world of the insane. But Doughty's relationship with Mohammed is the one bright spot of human feeling in the entire account of his travels. On one occasion, teased as being the son of a wolf, Doughty replies spiritedly: "'I am no wolfling, but weyladak, a son of thine.' 'Wellah,' answered the good man, surprised and smiling, 'thou art my son indeed'." Such moments, though, were few and far between. Doughty was not welcome, and when the messengers arrived back from Medina, their orders were that he was to proceed no further into the Hejaz, but to go back where he came from. His reception in Hail was unlikely to be enthusiastic, but Doughty was glad simply to get away from Kheybar.

He rode out of the town, accompanied by a bedu named Eyad, who had agreed to conduct him to Hail for five riyals, and by Mohammed, who accompanied him on foot a little of the way. The two friends shook hands, and then "the world, and death, and the inhumanity of religions parted us for ever". After a night in the desert, dawn came, and "oh joy! this sun being fairly risen, the abhorred landmarks of Kheybar appeared no more!"

Doughty's joy was shortlived. The journey itself was hard enough: they marched for hours across a volcanic plain without shade or water, until they found a small pond to fill their water-skins. "The water was full of wiggling white vermin; and we drank — giving God thanks — through a lap of our kerchiefs…"

If he had been in any doubt about his reception at Hail, the travellers they met on the way settled his mind for him. Ibn Rashid, they said, would kill him if he returned. But it was by no means certain that the Emir would have the chance: it was looking more and more as if Doughty's travelling companions might abandon him, or even do away with him on the road. In one fight, Doughty was beaten about the head and face after seizing the musket of one of his companions, who had been threatening to shoot him, and the little group moved on in surly silence, Doughty nursing a secret pistol inside the folds of his cloak.

Ibn Rashid himself was away from Hail on a raid, but that was small comfort for Doughty. People in the street looked askance at him, murmuring that perhaps this time he might be put to death, while the Emir's deputy, Aneybar, simply ordered him straight back to Kheybar. He might stay the night, he said, but then he must go. "He showed me these three pauses of his malicious wit on his fingers — Tomorrow! — The light! — Depart!" Neither Hail nor Kheybar would take him in, and either one would most certainly have him executed if he returned.

The companions who had brought him from Kheybar did not dare to take him back there. Instead, they said they had decided to take him to the village of Gofar, a few miles away — but in fact, it became clear, they intended to abandon him. They rode the camels, forcing Doughty to struggle along behind on foot. "My plight was such that I thought, after a few days of such efforts, I should rest for ever. So it drew to the burning midst of the afternoon when, what for the throes in my chest, I thought that the heart would burst. The hot blood at length spouted from my nostrils..."

So he struggled on, until finally his companions — who were, of course, in a predicament of their own, unable to defy the Dowla by obeying Aneybar's orders and taking him back to Kheybar — abandoned him at a small bedu encampment. His welcome there was hardly enthusiastic: one man threatened to chop off his head, another attacked him with a tent pole, while a third attacked him from behind with a sword. It was only the appeals of the women of the camp which saved his life, and persuaded the men to agree to find him a guide to take him to Boreyda, from where he might find a caravan to take him to the coast.

The man they found, named Hamad, had only just arrived in the region after a journey of one hundred and thirty miles from the west, and his preparations for the journey with Doughty, for which he was to be paid five riyals, speak volumes about the life of the desert bedu. In bedu fashion, he wasted neither provisions — all he took was a water-skin and a few handfuls of dried milk — nor words. "To his wife he said no more than this: 'Woman, I go with the stranger to Boreyda.' She obeyed silently; and commonly a bedu in departing bids not his wife farewell. 'Hearest thou?' said Hamad again. 'Follow with these Arabs until my coming home!' Then he took his little son in his arms and kissed him."

And with that, Doughty and his new *rafik* set out on their four hundred and fifty mile trek to Boreyda. Earlier, Doughty had buried his few books in the desert to lighten his load: "It is a free man that may carry all his worldly possession upon one of his shoulders," he said philosophically. Now he was started on another week's journey across the desert.

After struggling across the deep dunes of the Nefud where William Gifford Palgrave had all but foundered a few years before, the travellers came upon Boreyda almost like a mirage. "From hence appeared a dream-like spectacle! — a great clay town built in this waste sand with enclosing walls and towers and streets and houses! And there beside, a bluish dark wood of ethel trees, upon high dunes!" Surely now, Doughty thought, he must be able to find help to guide him to the coast and a ship home to Europe. Hamed's advice, like that of so many people before, that he should pretend to be a Muslim, might have caused him some foreboding; but if it did, it had little effect. Doughty ignored it as he had done on every previous occasion.

His refusal to join the evening prayers gave him away at once. "Art not thou the Nasrani that was lately at Hail...? Why then didst thou not go to Kheybar?" Doughty pretended that his camel had been too sick to travel further — but it was probably rivalry between the authorities of Boreyda and those of Hail which saved him. The sheikhs of Boreyda were only too pleased that the orders of Hail should have been ignored. Later, when the soldiers and slaves of the palace set about him, jostling, beating, and finally robbing him, the Emir's officer sprang to his defence, warning them that anyone who failed to return the property that had been stolen would have his hand chopped off.

But the experience had done little to smooth Doughty's tongue. When he was taken before the Emir himself, he was as outspoken as if he had been speaking to a kitchen boy. "Is it the custom here that strangers are robbed in the midst of your town? I have eaten of your bread and salt, and your servants set upon me in your yard," he complained — characteristically forgetting the officer's intervention on his behalf.

Word of the trouble in Hail and Kheybar had spread quickly, and the Emir wanted no repetition in Boreyda. Doughty, he said, must leave as soon as he had rested, and travel on to the nearby town of Aneyza. It was a wise decision: during the afternoon, a crowd came and stoned the house where Doughty was sleeping, while others were urging the Emir to have him put to death. But he was still under the protection of the Ottoman authorities: whatever might happen to him in the desert, the Emir was unwilling to take the risk of having him die in the town.

At first light, he was hustled out of the gates with a guide for the journey to Aneyza. They rode over the dunes, to avoid chance meetings with potentially unfriendly tribesmen, and by evening they were near the town. Doughty had been terrified all through the short journey that his guide would desert him; just outside Aneyza, he did just that. The Emir of the town, Zamil, was as uneasy about his presence as the leaders of Kheybar, Boreyda, and Hail had been, but at least he allowed Doughty to stay, although he warned him not to walk about in public. He was kindly treated by several of the wealthy merchants, but once again, he was driven out of the place where he was staying by an angry mob.

After a few weeks, with feeling against him increasing by the day, he was woken at night, and under cover of darkness taken to a palm grove outside the town, where he would be permitted to stay. He could no longer travel into Aneyza, but his friends sent him food, and finally found him a place on a merchants' caravan taking butter to Mecca. It was a step in the right direction, and although the journey was long and hard, there was relief from the blazing desert heat as the party climbed into the mountains. At five thousand feet, Doughty noted, the air was light and refreshing, and the countryside spread with grass — "the best wild pasture land that I have ever seen in Arabia".

Three weeks of travelling brought the party to the approaches of Mecca: Doughty, as a non-Muslim, could go no further, until the leaders of a small local caravan agreed to escort him to Taif. Once again, he had no way of knowing whether he would be welcomed, shut out of the city, or simply put to death; certainly, several of the company with which he was travelling had no doubt about their preference. Their only doubt was whether the Sheriff at Taif should have Doughty hanged, or simply cut off his head. But even in this atmosphere of hatred, the traveller was able to rely on the tradition of hospitality. His pistol was found and taken from him, leaving him defenceless, but again and again, he reminded his companions that he had eaten bread and salt with them, and that therefore it would be a crime against the desert code for them to attack him.

It was, to say the least, an uneasy journey, but as they came closer to Taif, there were paved stretches of road, and passages blasted through the rock faces. They were coming closer to the centre of Ottoman power in Arabia. When they arrived, Doughty must have presented a pathetic sight. "The tunic was rent on my back, my mantle was old and torn; the hair was grown down under my kerchief to the shoulders, and the beard fallen and unkempt. I had bloodshot eyes, half blinded, and the scorched skin was cracked to the quick upon my face," he wrote.

The Sheriff, Hasseyn Pasha, welcomed him almost like royalty. He was anxious to have no trouble with foreign governments, and the safest course seemed to him to look after Doughty as well as he could, before escorting him down to the coast, onto a ship, and away. After four days in Taif, the wanderer was on his way again, this time to Jeddah and a ship which would take him to Aden, to India, and then home to England. He had been travelling around Arabia for two years.

Even at home, Doughty's troubles were not over. Five years' work on his account of his travels ended with a manuscript which publishers in England dismissed as 'hardly intelligible' and which, when it was eventually published, made a loss. Perhaps worse, his fellow-travellers disagreed about him: Burton, for instance, dismissed him as a charlatan, a bigot, and a coward.

Only Wilfrid Blunt regarded him as having "the most complete knowledge among Englishmen of Arabian things", while other writers praised his scientist's regard for the details of natural phenomena on his travels.

However, it was knowledge untempered with sympathy or humility. Doughty was harsh, arrogant, opinionated and provocative, and it is easy to see how tribesmen and villagers alike must have been provoked by him. And yet, *Travels in Arabia Deserta* remains a haunting book. Blunt's verdict that it was 'the best ever written' may be excessively enthusiastic, but it did at least bring the cruel realities of bedu life home to a public in England whose view of the Orient was rosy and romanticised. Of all the travel writers who wandered through Arabia, Doughty may well take the prize as the worst-prepared and least obliging traveller — but he must also be given credit as by far the most poetic and imaginative writer.

Valley of Diamonds, Plains of Gold

"There is nothing so noble as to travel and make friends"

– Mohammed ibn Aruk

Wilfrid Scawen Blunt, poet, diplomat, political agitator, traveller, and libertine, knew little of modesty and understatement, and when he described the reason for the journey he and his wife made across Arabia's Great Nefud desert, it was in ringing tones that were clearly meant for posterity. "It is hardly an exaggeration… to speak of it as a pilgrimage… though the religion in whose name we travelled was only one of romance," he declared grandly.

Blunt's whole life was lived, as it were, at full volume; from his barely-concealed amorous intrigues to his political campaigning, everything seemed to have been designed for an audience. And yet his credentials as a friend of the Arabs are impeccable: he fought all his life for Arab nationalism, was banned from British-ruled Egypt for his activities, and imprisoned briefly as a spy by the authorities of the Ottoman Empire.

But for all his pre-occupation with the realities of Arab politics, he shared enthusiastically in the myths of his time about Arabia. The Blunts travelled at least partly in search of the picture-book exoticism with which Victorian England invested the Arab world. They took little interest in the ordinary Arabs they came across; the ones who guided them, advised them, or offered them their hospitality. The ones they were anxious to meet were those who corresponded to their own romantic preconceptions: powerful sheikhs, pure-bred bedu warriors, or those like their friend Mohammed ibn Aruk, who could spin a pretty tale of noble relatives, travel, and the misery of separation.

The Blunts carried with them an overwhelming sense of their own social importance. In their accounts of their travels, they each seize delightedly upon anything that can be related to the *Tales of the Arabian Nights*, or described in the self-consciously poetic language of romance: a desert wadi is likened to Sindbad's Valley of Diamonds, and the pair discuss only half-jokingly the likelihood of having their heads struck off in an angry potentate's fit of pique. They drew maps of the terrain as they travelled through it, and made notes of the animals and plants they saw, but the journey they really hoped to make was away from reality and into the realm of myth and fairyland.

Blunt shared, too, in the self-denying hardiness that has marked most of Arabia's explorers. His life away from the desert was one of almost obsessive self-indulgence, and yet he wrote wistfully of "the pleasures of an outdoor life which is too soberly severe for folly, a life of bodily toil, of an abstemious habit in meat and drink, rough lying on the ground by night, and endurance of sun, wind and rain by day..."

Part of the self-conscious romance of their expedition lay in its immediate objective: to accompany their former travelling-companion, now grandiloquently styled Blunt's blood-brother, on a journey back to the land of his ancestors, in order to meet his distant relatives, and maybe even help him find a wife. It was a journey that the Blunts, with their own obsessions about their breeding and high birth, could contemplate with excitement — a journey into a world of pure-bred bedu tribesmen and the sheikhly sons of ancient desert families.

It's to be hoped, perhaps, that their hosts and companions occasionally laughed at them behind their hands — because the Blunts most certainly never smiled at themselves.

For an English aristocrat, grand-daughter of Lord Byron, and descendant, or so she claimed, of Alfred the Great, the Plantagenets, and the Emperor Charlemagne, the Lady Anne Blunt wrote with supreme confidence of the subtleties of camel trading. "In choosing camels," she said, "the principal points to look at are breadth of chest, depth of barrel, shortness of leg, and for condition, roundness of flank. I have seen the strength of the hocks tested by a man standing on them while the camel is kneeling. If it can rise, despite the weight, there can be no doubt as to soundness…"

Like many of the European adventurers in Arabia, her expertise came simply from listening carefully to her Arab companion; but as she checked over the camels in Damascus's Maidan district, she noted with a housewife's care the price of the animals which were to carry her and her husband on their expedition to search for the pure-bred Arab horses of Nejd. They were "strong enough to carry away the gates of Gaza" — and they cost a mere ten pounds each.

The real camel expert was the Blunts' friend, Mohammed ibn Aruk, from the town of Tudmur — the modern Palmyra — who had accompanied them on earlier journeys in the Arab world, and who now wanted to travel south to the Nejd region of Saudi Arabia, from which his family had originally sprung. He had the names of some of his relatives, and he knew the towns where they lived; now, with the Blunts, he would travel to visit them. For the Blunts themselves, it was the start of one of the greatest adventures of their lives — a journey of a thousand miles or so through some of the harshest country in the world, to an area which Blunt described as 'the cradle of the Bedouins' race'.

It was Friday, December 13, 1878 when the Blunts finally took their last look back at the houses and minarets of Damascus, a date which Blunt declared left him 'superstitious and full of dark forebodings'. Their pace was leisurely enough for the first few days, as they progressed through the small towns that lay in their way, for all the world like Victorian gentlefolk of quality leaving their calling cards behind them.

Christmas was almost upon them before they were ready to move on from Salkhad. "Tomorrow we may hope to sleep in the desert," reads Lady Anne's journal, and then, a few hours after: "A white frost, and off at half past seven." Three days later, on Christmas Eve, they were sitting shivering outside their tents in a chill evening wind, eating a festive supper of curry and tinned plum pudding. They had made painfully slow progress over a flat plain covered with black volcanic boulders, which made the camels stumble and lose their footing, and had slowed them to around two miles an hour, but they had at least plenty of supplies, and the wadis were full of water.

Even so, they were glad enough after a couple of days of a chance addition to their diet — a swarm of red locusts which took to the air as the morning sun began to warm the ground, enabling the Blunts' entourage to pursue them, knocking them out of the air with their sticks. "The locusts, fried, are fairly good to eat," noted Lady Anne, more adventurous than Palgrave, but still with something less than a gourmet's zeal for a new taste. Later in her journey, she was to become more enthusiastic, and even offer the curious reader a recipe for the preparation of the giant insects: "They are best plain boiled. The legs must be pulled off and the locust held by the wings, dipped into salt, and eaten. As to flavour, this insect tastes of vegetable rather than fish or flesh..."

In fact, the locusts, or *jarad*, were a perennial curse and blessing upon the Arabs. They could strip a date plantation in a few hours, leaving the hard-pressed farmers without a harvest — and yet their fattened and fried bodies provided a favourite delicacy. A few years before the Blunts, Charles Doughty had observed: "The *jarad* devour the bedu, and the bedu devour the *jarad*...", words which, he flattered himself, were later treated as a proverb.

The Blunts struck their tents in the chilly first moments of the dawn, and made their way southwards down the Wadi Sirhan, a level plain of sand and grit, pressing on after a breakfast of coffee and dry biscuit until three or four in the afternoon. As they rode, they would nibble occasionally at dates and hard rusk, but there were no halts until it was time to pitch their tents again. "It is wonderful how little food one can do with while travelling. We have had no meat now for the last four days till today, only beef tea and burghal, and dates, with sometimes fried onions, or flour mixed with curry powder and butter, and baked into a cake…"

Mohammed passed the time by gleefully telling them the story of how he was lost in the desert as a boy and almost died of thirst; a party of camel men who found him took him at first for a slave, because the sun had burned him so black, but when one of the party recognised him, they gave him water. Had he really been a slave, perhaps he might have been less lucky.

The Blunts' various guides, perhaps understandably, seemed to enjoy describing the possible horrors of the desert to their European companions, but the risks of the present journey were about to become plain enough. They were attacked by robbers on a *ghazu*, or raid, who galloped up on horses as the Blunts were pausing near a well. "They all turned on Wilfrid, who had waited for me, some of them jumping down on foot to get hold of his mare's halter… At last his assailants managed to get his gun from him and broke it over his head, hitting him three times and smashing the stock. Resistance seemed to me useless, and I shouted to the nearest horseman, '*Ana dahilak*' (I am under your protection), the usual form of surrender," wrote Lady Anne later. The rest of the party were by now sheltering behind their camels, with their guns pointed nervously towards the robber band, and it was only when they explained who they were, who the Blunts were, and who their friends were, that the matter was resolved.

It was the Blunts' first acquaintance with the law of the desert, and with the complex system of *rabia*, or companions, on which all the desert travellers were to rely, and which largely replaced the rule of the powerless authorities of the Ottoman Empire. The robbers were Ruaulla, a tribe allied to Mohammed's Tudmuri family — and paying tribute, besides, to an Arab sheikh with whom the Blunts had stayed on an earlier journey. Once the network of loyalties and family connections was established, the mares, the gun, and even Wilfrid's tobacco pouch were handed back to their owners, though not without a few wry faces on the part of the Arabs who had briefly been their new owners. "We were all on very good terms, sitting in a circle on the sand, eating dates and passing round the pipe of peace. They were now our guests."

Lady Anne was understandably relieved — and even more bewildered. "What struck us as strange in all this was the really good faith with which they believed every word we said. We had spoken the truth, but why did they trust us? They knew neither us nor Mohammed, yet they had taken our word that we were friends, when they might so easily have ridden off without question with our property. Nobody would ever have heard of it, or known who they were."

It was a bemusement with the Arab system of honour that other travellers were to share. Later in their journey, the Blunts heard of the law enforcement policies of the Emir Mohammed ibn Rashid at Hail, who would briskly lop off the heads of strangers found loafing around near the roads in his domain as an example to anyone thinking of mounting an armed attack on passing travellers. It was, Lady Anne says convincingly, an effective policy — there had been no robberies on the Emir's highways for years — and yet the self-imposed traditional law of the desert bedu might seem to have been both more civilised and just as effective, if a little less romantic.

After the adventure of the *ghazu*, the party set off again at a brisk pace: away by seven in the morning, and a thirty-mile march without pausing. They had decided to cut straight across the dusty gravel plain towards Jof, a route that offered little water, and correspondingly little chance of another raid by travelling robbers. The Blunts, perhaps wisely, weren't anxious to try their luck with desert law for a second time. From their camp that night by a rocky outcrop of red, yellow, and purple sandstone, they could see a distant blue line of hills. The hills lay beyond the town of Jof, their guides told them, and they marked the edge of the Great Nefud desert.

The town itself, clustered around a forbidding black castle, lay in a natural rocky basin, some three miles across. It was, Lady Anne concluded, no doubt the site of a small inland sea, presumably once fed from the Wadi Sirhan, down which they had travelled. Outside the walls were a few square patches of young green corn. "They are watered from wells, and irrigated just like the gardens inside the walls, with little water-courses carefully traced in patterns, like a jam tart."

This was the town in which Mohammed was to look for the first of his long-lost relatives and, although he seemed unclear about the precise nature of the relationship, the entire party was welcomed to a feast, with a young lamb killed in honour of the travellers.

For the Blunts, concerned as they were about pedigree, status, and social standing, the governor of Jof presented something of an enigma. "He is a negro slave, we are told, but a person of great consequence, and a personal friend of the Emir," noted Lady Anne with some concern. Fortunately, he was away at the town of Meskakeh, so they had no need to wrestle with the social problems of handling a man of such confusing rank.

But they were well pleased with their reception, first by Mohammed's relatives, and then by the officials who invited them to stay in the governor's castle, and they took the opportunity to make their calls on the town's notables. "At all the houses we were fed and entertained, having to drink endless cups of coffee flavoured with cloves, and eat innumerable dates, the helwet el Jof, which they say here are the best in Arabia. They are of excellent flavour, but too sweet and too sticky for general use," Lady Anne wrote in her diary.

After three days, they moved on to Meskakeh, some twenty miles away, and the last town of any size before the red sands of the Great Nefud desert. With them travelled a number of people from Jof, including an old man who carried water in an ostrich shell slung in a net over his shoulder. Ostriches, he told them, were common enough in the desert they were approaching.

"The scenery all the way was fantastic, even picturesque... In the wadis where water had flowed, for it rained here about a month ago, there were bright green bulbous plants with crocus flowers, giving a false look of fertility," Lady Anne wrote.

The surrounding countryside, startling though as it was, corrected that false first impression. Much of it was absolutely barren and covered with salt; mushroom-shaped rocks of pink sandstone topped with the red stains of iron ore deposits dotted the plain, and there were sandhills and outlying rocky crags, with high distant mountains on all sides.

Like Jof, Meskakeh was dominated by its ancient citadel, but the main interest of the travellers was in finding the home of the ibn Aruks of Meskakeh, the main branch of the family Mohammed had come to rediscover, and from among whom he hoped to find a bride. The Blunts, who had grown used to the tales and exaggerations of their friend, were slightly surprised to find that the family actually existed — although they proved a little too ordinary for the refined tastes of the aristocratic Lady Anne. "Like their relations of Tudmur, they have been too long settled as mere townspeople, marrying the daughters of the land, and adopting many of the sordid town notions. But they were honest and kind-hearted, and the traditions of their origin, still religiously preserved, cast an occasional gleam of something like romance on their otherwise matter-of-fact lives," she said condescendingly.

Nevertheless, they deigned to stay with these ordinary folk for three days, receiving their open-handed hospitality and, much more important, conducting the delicate negotiations over Mohammed's choice of a bride. That, of course, was a job for Lady Anne herself, and she immersed herself in it with relish.

Their host, Nassr, had a cousin, Jazi, with two unmarried daughters, and it was on Jazi's wife that she paid her visit. She cast a cold eye on the two sisters: Asr, the elder, seemed shy, bad-tempered, and rude, but her young sister, Muttra, made a better impression. "I was pleased with the intelligence she showed in conversation, and pleased with her pretty ways and honest face, and I decided in my own mind without difficulty that Mohammed would be most fortunate if he obtained her in marriage," she said.

Muttra had passed Lady Anne's searching examination, and now the only haggling would be over the price of the dowry. Or so Lady Anne believed.

But Jazi wanted to bargain: first the bride-price went up from forty to sixty pounds, and then he dropped his bombshell — rather than the easy-going, amicable Muttra, he wanted Mohammed to accept her elder sister, Asr. A family council was called, with Blunt sitting in to represent Mohammed, and Muttra finally became his betrothed, for a dowry predictably half-way between the asking and the offered price. The cultured Lady Anne wisely kept her feelings to herself: "It was not very dignified, this chaffering about price; and people do better in England, leaving such things to their lawyers."

The other negotiation in Meskakeh was to arrange official permission from the governor, Johar, to continue on to Hail; although the Blunts deliberately eschewed disguise for their journeys, they were not above employing a little deception to get their way. Mohammed had been briefed to present a story of visiting friends — "of course not by any means the whole truth, but true as far as it went," Lady Anne explains delicately — and, with the bargaining oiled by the gift of some handsome clothes to the governor and a small bribe, the party was allowed to proceed.

It was perhaps just as well. "As Wilfrid remarked, when we were well on our mares again and riding home, Johar was just the picture of a capricious despot, and one who, if he had been in a bad humour, might have ordered our heads off with no more ceremony than he had ordered breakfast..."

Now was to come the climax of their journey, and they agreed to choose the more difficult route across the Great Nefud, with its high dunes and treacherous deep sands, simply to see the country at its worst. It would mean ten days' hard travelling, with only two wells on the whole two-hundred mile route. "We hear wonderful accounts of it here, and of the people who have been lost in it," wrote Lady Anne, with perhaps a rather surprising enthusiasm. "We shall need all our strength for the next ten days." Mohammed's tales of horror and deprivation had obviously only whetted her appetite.

The Blunts' expectations and apprehensions about the Great Nefud had been coloured by their reading of William Gifford Palgrave's account of his own impressions there as a French spy 16 years earlier. For him, the burning walls of sand were clearly a nightmare glimpse of hell: but this was the country into which they were travelling, the object of their dreams, said Lady Anne, throughout their journey.

As the palm groves of Meskakeh vanished over the horizon behind them, they found themselves struggling over dunes of pure white sand, sometimes a hundred feet or more high, until they reached a little group of seventy or so houses, scattered around a rocky mound topped by a ruined castle. It was the village of Kara, the last human habitation they would see for days. A few miles further on, they laboured up a steep rocky slope, to break out not into the red sands of the Nefud, but onto a wide, gravelly plain stretching southwards to the horizon. It was only after a few more hours' travel that they saw on the horizon the red streak of the desert.

"On coming nearer, we found it broken into billows, and but for its red colour not unlike a stormy sea seen from the shore, for it rose up, as the sea seems to rise, when the waves are high, above the level of the land," wrote Lady Anne.

The two travellers cantered together up to the edge of the sand, and looked out for a few moments over the great red desert of central Arabia, their mares' feet buried in the first waves of the rolling sand sea. It was its colour which struck them first — like rhubarb and magnesia, they suggested, and almost crimson in the morning with the dew on it. And, even more surprising, given Palgrave's warnings, it was far from barren. Ghada bushes and stunted yerta trees with long knotted stems grew up all over it, making it better wooded and richer in pasture than any other part of the desert they had passed through. All it lacked was water — and that, for the bedu who followed their camels for weeks at a time, living off their milk, was no difficulty. They, though, would wait for the spring, when the grass was green after rain: in mid-winter, the Blunts saw hardly anyone along their route.

They had little time for Palgrave and his burning walls of sand: his descriptions, said Blunt himself tartly later, bore "very little resemblance to the reality". But within a few days, their own discoveries bore witness to the terrible cruelty of the landscape — dry bones, often of camels, but sometimes of men and horses, lay half-covered by the blowing sand where they had fallen. Radi, the companion sent with them from Meskakeh, told them an even more gruesome story, of five hundred Turkish soldiers abandoned in the desert by their guides. Their bones, he said, were found scattered around the bushes in the sand, and their horses, which made their way back to civilisation, were eventually sold off by the locals for a few sheep or goats each.

There was, though, one meeting which gave Mohammed and Blunt himself a chance to prove their bravery to each other after the debacle of the earlier *ghazu*. They spotted half a dozen people camped at the bottom of a depression, with a few camels grazing nearby; as they rode down to investigate, the camp broke up in a frenzy of activity. "As soon as they saw us, the women ran and pulled the tent down, while the men rushed off to the nearest camels, and made them kneel. They were evidently in a fright," wrote Lady Anne. "The Arabs take pride in being able to strike camp and march at almost a moment's notice, and in this case, I think it hardly took three minutes."

Far from being a threat, they were a group of poor bedu, scared for their camels and their lives by the sudden approach of the strangers. But, with the constant effort of dragging through the ankle-deep sand beginning to tell on men, horses, and camels alike, the Blunts were more anxious now about the way that lay ahead than about the possibility of attack. Perhaps it was not the best time for Radi to choose to tell them that no heavily-laden caravan like theirs had ever crossed the Nefud by that route before.

Blunt himself made a short speech to the whole party about the serious nature of their predicament — not, surely, something that needed explaining — and announced that water rations were to be doled out in the evening. There was to be no water drunk during the day. It was the guide though, old and physically unimpressive as they may have found him, who saved their lives. He sat for hours in silence on the back of his horse, "an ancient bag of bones which looks as if it would never last through the journey", occasionally pointing with a shrivelled finger at the way they were to take. "He is a curious little old man, as dry and black and withered as the dead stumps of the yerta bushes one sees here, the driftwood of the Nefud" — but he was still a mine of information about the strange landscape through which they were travelling.

He described to them the secret wildlife of the desert, the creatures which lived there but were seldom seen, including what sounded like a cobra, a snake which "stands on its tail, and sticks out its neck like wings". There were small birds, kestrels, and desert hares, and even the tracks of antelope, animals which Radi declared never left the Nefud and never drank. Later in the journey, the hot sun brought a huge tarantula spider out from its hiding place in the sands, the only venomous creature they saw on the entire expedition.

But more important than his zoological expertise was his flawless sense of direction. He found his way, apparently, almost entirely by landmarks, either natural features of the landscape, or piles of dry wood he had painstakingly set up on earlier journeys at the summit of each hill. At the same time, it gradually became clear that he was following a track used by other travellers as well.

"We have learned to make out a sort of road after all, of an intermittent kind, marked by the dung of camels, and occasionally on the side of a steep slope, there is a distinct footway," wrote Lady Anne. But neither the Blunts nor their other Arab companions could have found their way alone. To them, they admitted, each sand-hill looked like the one before and the one after. Understandably, their faith in their guide occasionally wavered as they plodded on for mile after weary mile, and it was not until they spotted the conical rocky peaks of Aalem on the horizon that they were finally convinced that the worst was over, and that they were truly on the way to Jobba. On the rocks, they spotted a butterfly sunning itself, one of the tiny but intriguing mysteries of their journey. "If, as is probable, there is no vegetation suitable for a caterpillar nearer than Hebron, this little insect must have travelled at least four hundred miles," Lady Anne mused.

The struggle through the sands was perceptibly weakening the camels, and water was running short. There was no fresh pasture for them; last year's grass was white and withered with no sign of life or nourishment, and there was no new growth. After a week's journeying, the pace of the caravan had slowed until they were travelling at barely one mile an hour. An overnight thunderstorm had briefly wetted and hardened the sands for them, and but for that piece of luck, they might well not have survived.

The Blunts themselves, Lady Anne admitted, were by far the weakest of the party, unable to struggle through the sand on foot for long for lack of breath or strength. "Neither of us could have kept up on foot," she wrote blithely, later. "But a European is no match for even a town Arab in the matter of walking. At one moment, it seemed as if we should remain altogether in the Nefud, adding a new chapter to old Radi's tales of horror... The sand to tired camels is like a prison, and in the sand we should have remained."

But the track was getting clearer; there were regular cuttings at some places, and Radi was adamant that there was a road of stone running under the sands. Best of all, though, was the sudden sight of the group of hills on the horizon which they knew were the rocks of Jobba, the oasis for which they were heading. From there, it was still several miles to the village, but it was on harder ground, and all downhill. They had successfully crossed Arabia's Great Nefud; they could pause and rest, and the town of Hail was only a few days' march further on.

But after the nightmares of solitude came the dangers of society. At Jobba, the Blunts found themselves the object of unwelcome interest. "I dare say they meant no harm, but the manners of the young people of the village were bad, and there was something almost hostile in their tone about Nasrani which it was advisable to check," wrote Lady Anne, with the tone of a village schoolmistress. It was, she pointed out, the only religious animosity they had felt in their entire journey — a happy contrast with Charles Doughty's experience — but it made them nervous about what they should expect at Hail.

Crossing the Nafud had been the Blunts' great adventure, but it had also been a moment of decision. From now on, there was nothing they could do but travel on to Hail where they mistakenly believed no undisguised European or Christian had ever been, and see what reception they would get from the Emir Mohammed ibn Rashid, the richest and most powerful ruler of all Arabia.

The journey now was easy, with the weary camels cropping their fill of the plentiful new shoots of nassi grass, and the Blunts and their Arab companions singing and playing in the soft sand like children as they went along. The reaction of the Arabs to Wilfrid Blunt's parlour-game sense of fun can only be imagined. "Bedouins," said his wife primly, "never play at games…" and then she went on to describe her husband turning three times round with his head resting on a short stick, and then trying to walk straight. The bemused Arabs must have been convinced that the eccentric and bombastic Englishman had finally gone mad with the heat.

As they got closer to the Arab town, so their concern increased. "Wilfrid declares he shall die happy now, even if we have our heads cut off in Hail," says Lady Anne's journal, bravely but not entirely convincingly. They sent on ahead of them letters of introduction to the Emir, though, and were greeted in the courtyard of the castle at Hail by a tall, white-bearded old man who came solemnly forward towards them.

"The Emir!" Mohammed whispered to them, in awe.

Their welcome, said the punctilious Lady Anne, was all they could have desired. At last they had met a person of genuine quality, even though Lady Anne, probably influenced by the stories she had heard of the murders by which he had fought his way to his position of power, thought him fearful and conscience-stricken, like some Arab Richard III.

Whatever her fancies, they themselves were treated with the respect and regard they felt to be their due; offered their own lodging near the castle walls, received privately by the Emir, and shown around his private palm groves, where gazelles, antelopes, and ibex wandered about among the trees. Lady Anne was invited into the Emir's harem, where she seems to have gazed about her like a tourist at clothes, jewellery and wall-hangings, but to have had little time for the women she found there. "They have no idea of amusement, if I may judge from what they said to me, but a firm conviction that perfect happiness and dignity consist in sitting still," she noted acerbicly.

Ibn Rashid's stud, which he showed off to them within hours of their arrival, was the most celebrated in Arabia, although the Blunts agreed privately that they were rather disappointed with the quality of his horses. But the Emir had surprises for his guests — among them, ironically, the first telephone they had ever seen — "one of those toys which were the fashion last year in Europe", said Lady Anne dismissively, determined not to be impressed by the unwelcome modernity of her romantic Arabian idyll.

And then, suddenly, their welcome cooled. Miffed, the Blunts discovered that they were no longer being treated like honoured guests. "The presents of game ceased, and the lamb, with which we had hitherto been regaled at dinner, was replaced by camel meat. Instead of two soldiers being sent to escort us to the palace, a slave boy came with a message…"

One has the feeling, reading Lady Anne's list of complaints, that the dramatic despatch Wilfrid had foreseen at the hands of the Emir's executioner might almost have been more welcome than this debilitating social death. But the reason was not far to seek: Mohammed, it seemed, had been exaggerating his own importance in talks with the Emir, and at the same time, belittling that of his companions and employers. It was all right, apparently, for Wilfrid to amuse himself by dubbing him a blood-brother, but matters had gone too far when he claimed social superiority. Blunt seized the bull by the horns, and had the whole unfortunate matter explained to the Emir. "It would not have been worth mentioning," declared Lady Anne condescendingly, "except as an illustration of Arab manners and ways of thought" — although Mohammed, the Emir, and the members of his entourage might have found it also an interesting sidelight on the manners, ways of thought, and sensibilities of English gentlefolk.

The slight unpleasantness associated with the misunderstanding encouraged the Blunts to leave the palace a little earlier than they might otherwise have done, and resume their travels. They spent a few days more there, with the Emir, once more all politeness and attention, sending them on a visit to his mountain fortress of Agde. They were treated on the way to a ringing Shammar war-song from their bedu companions:

> *Ma arid ana erkobu delul,*
> *Lau zeynuli shedadeha,*
> *Aridu ana hamra shenuf,*
> *Hamra seryeh aruddeha…*
> (I would not ride a mere delul,
> Though lovely to me her shedad;
> Let me be mounted on a mare,
> A bay mare, swift and quick to turn….)

Here, perhaps, was a welcome glimpse of the romantic Arabia the Blunts were looking for: galloping across the sands with fierce bedu warriors for their companions, and a secret castle in the hills, with fertile wadis below it. It was, Lady Anne noted delightedly, like Sindbad's Valley of Diamonds in the *Arabian Nights* — and, to put the final seal of approval on it for the cost-conscious Blunts, it was all free. "If we had been in Turkey, or anywhere else in Arabia, we should have had to give a handsome tip after an expedition of this kind — but at Hail nothing of the sort was expected…"

After describing their farewell, in which they declined the Emir's offers of gifts, camels, or even one of his prize mares, Lady Anne rather ungratefully noted: "Our heads had been in the jaws of the lion long enough, and now our only object was to get quietly and decorously out of the den." They said their goodbyes, and rode quietly away with one glance back at the 'lion's den' where they had been so well and so hospitably received. Before them lay one of the most beautiful vistas they had ever seen: a foreground of coarse reddish sand, scattered with clumps of huge pollarded ithel trees, some of them thirty feet around. Across the sand was a broad green belt of barley, and beyond that, the desert faded away from red to orange, to disappear into what looked like a shining blue sheet of water. Away in the distance, seeming to wade through the water of the mirage, and each one apparently reflected in it, was the long line of returning Haj pilgrims, making their way slowly homewards towards Persia; behind them, the sapphire-coloured crags of Jebel Aja shimmering in the desert sun.

For this part of their journey, they joined the pilgrim caravan which was returning from Mecca, although once again, the niceties of Victorian life sat uncomfortably with the habits of the desert. "They have an unpleasant habit of washing in the water first, and drinking it afterwards, which we are told is part of their religious ritual," sniffed Lady Anne. "Our camp tonight is a pleasanter one than yesterday's, being farther from the pilgrims."

Splitting up from the main body of the Haj, they made their way northwards, back across the scrub-covered fringes of the same Nefud desert they had crossed earlier with such difficulty, occasionally shooting a bird to vary their diet, until shortage of water forced them back to the main route. There was little comfort there, though: large parties of bedu had gathered at the wells of Khuddra, many of them with spears, and although they left the European travellers to themselves, they seemed surly and unwelcoming. Like other travellers before and after them, the Blunts were amazed at how news of their presence had spread among the tribes: the bedu had heard not just of them, but more particularly of the twelve-shot repeater rifle they had given to the Emir as a gift.

The water itself sounds less than appetising, as indeed it must often have been from the desert wells. "The wells are seventy feet deep, and the water when first drawn smells of rotten eggs; but the smell goes off on exposure to the air," wrote Lady Anne stoically.

The local tribes, too, were in great distress because of the failure of the autumn rains. Even so, and despite the apparent unfriendliness of the tribesmen at the wells, the Blunts were entertained with all the generosity the bedu could muster when they visited a camp. They were offered tumin, fresh butter and camel's milk, while inside the tents they could see great piles of locusts, dried over the fire, and ready to eat. But for the swarms of locusts, it seemed the Arabs would have starved.

Once out of the Nefud, the pace quickened as the Haj hurried on over broken stony ground at a pace of around three miles an hour, without any stops along the way. The pilgrims by now were feeling some anxiety, as they had barely travelled half the journey, and their provisions were all but exhausted. Despite this, the leader of the caravan forced a delay while he collected contributions from the pilgrims for himself.

After the march restarted, there were the first signs of weakness among the Blunts' party: one of the camels that had travelled with them from Damascus proved too weak to struggle to the top of a hill, and was left behind, grazing fitfully in a wadi bottom. His chances of survival were slim, and his predicament caused Lady Anne a pang of sympathy. "I shall not easily forget his face, looking wistfully after his

Pilgrims returning to Cairo, *Carl Haag, 1894. Cairo, like Damascus, was an important meeting place for the Haj. The arrival there would mean an end to months of hardship. (Mathaf Gallery)*

Overleaf: Arrival of the Caravan, Khan Asad Pasha, Damascus, *Charles Robertson. Many of the early travellers hid themselves among the huge trading caravans. (Mathaf Gallery)*

TRAVELS

IN

ARABIA,

COMPREHENDING AN ACCOUNT

OF THOSE TERRITORIES IN HEDJAZ WHICH

THE MOHAMMEDANS REGARD AS SACRED.

BY THE LATE

JOHN LEWIS BURCKHARDT.

PUBLISHED BY AUTHORITY OF

THE ASSOCIATION FOR PROMOTING THE DISCOVERY OF

THE INTERIOR OF AFRICA.

IN TWO VOLUMES.

VOL. I.

LONDON:

HENRY COLBURN, NEW BURLINGTON STREET.

1829.

The title page to Burckhardt's Travels in Arabia, *1829. (Bodleian Library)*

Above: The ancient Nabataean stone city of Petra which built its prosperity on the trade routes through Arabia. Burckhardt was the first scholar to identify the ruins of the city. (Andrew Taylor)

Left: The Treasury at Petra. (Andrew Taylor)

Halte d'une Caravane, *Charles Th. Frère. Burckhardt would have done much of his travelling in a caravan such as this. (Mathaf Gallery)*

Overleaf: Raid on a Caravan, Ghazu, *H Wood. A modern view of one of the sudden raids which traders and pilgrims alike might suffer. (Mathaf Gallery)*

Above: Burton's litter. (Bodleian Library)

Right: Burton, dressed as 'Sheikh Abdullah' from Afghanistan, rode in a litter partly because of a swollen and infected foot. But it also made it easier to maintain his disguise. (Bodleian Library)

CAPTAIN
SIR RICHARD FRANCIS
BURTON.
K.C.M.G. F.R.G.S.
BORN 19 MARCH
1821
DIED AT TRIESTE
20 OCTOBER
1890.

R · I · P

ISABEL
HIS WIFE,
NÉE ARUNDELL
(OF WARDOUR)
DIED 22ND DAY OF
MARCH 1896.

R · I · P

JESUS MERCY MARY HELP
PRAY FOR HER.

RICHARD BURTON

"FAREWELL,DEAR FRIEND,DEAD HERO!THE GREAT LIFE
IS ENDED,THE GREAT PERILS,THE GREAT JOYS:
AND HE TO WHOM ADVENTURES WERE AS TOYS,
WHO SEEMED TO BEAR A CHARM 'GAINST SPEAR OR KNIFE
OR BULLET, NOW LIES SILENT FROM ALL STRIFE
OUT YONDER WHERE THE AUSTRIAN EAGLES POISE
ON ISTRIAN HILLS.BUT ENGLAND,AT THE NOISE
OF THAT DREAD FALL,WEEPS WITH THE HERO'S WIFE.
OH,LAST AND NOBLEST OF THE ERRANT KNIGHTS,
THE ENGLISH SOLDIER AND THE ARAB SHIEK!
OH,SINGER OF THE EAST WHO LOVED SO WELL
THE DEATHLESS WONDER OF THE 'ARABIAN NIGHTS,'
WHO TOUCHED CAMOEN'S LUTE AND STILL WOULD SEEK
EVER NEW DEEDS UNTIL THE END!FAREWELL!"

JUSTIN HUNTLY McCARTHY.

Sir Richard Burton's tomb in Mortlake Catholic Cemetery, near London. His widow had to raise the money from friends to pay for his marble replica of an Arab tent. (Pippa McCarthy)

Right: A Caravan Approaching an Oasis, *Charles Th Frère (1814-1888). It was at the oases and watering-holes that the caravans were at their most vulnerable. (Mathaf Gallery)*

An Arab Encampment, *Eugene Alexis Girardet.* "As we sat about the evening fire, he brought me a bowl of their evening milk, made hot… I blessed him, and said it was the best of all nourishment," *Charles Doughty. (Mathaf Gallery)*

Charles Montagu Doughty, *Eric Kennington, 1921. Doughty said the sun had made him an Arab and, although he remained constantly hostile to Arab ways and Arab thoughts, his account of his travels is the most graphic description of the inner, spiritual journey of an Arabian traveller. (National Portrait Gallery, London)*

companions as they disappeared over the crest of the hill. He is the first of our small party that has fallen out of the ranks, and we are depressed with the feeling that he may not be the last," she wrote.

The camels of the Haj were looking painfully thin, weary with forced marches, and not allowed by their riders to graze as they went along: unlike the desert tribesmen the riders had only hired them for the journey from their bedu owners, and apparently cared nothing for their welfare. Within a few days, dozens of the animals had died while slowly, painfully, the struggling pilgrims made their way into Nejef.

The hardest part of the journey was over, both for the pilgrims and for the Blunts. The pilgrims would now split up to make their way home to their own countries, and a few days later, in Baghdad, the Blunts' entourage also set out for home.

For Wilfrid, and Lady Anne, though, there were more journeys in prospect: "Amongst the letters awaiting our arrival in Baghdad, we had found an invitation from Lord and Lady Lytton to spend the summer with them at Simla," wrote Lady Anne, with a degree of social triumph. Arabia was behind them: Persia, the Gulf, and a slightly more conventional brand of polite society, lay before.

Further ahead, of course, lay more travels, more adventures, and more disasters. Over the next forty-four years, Blunt's peculiar mixture of self-importance, obstinacy, rebelliousness and courage were to take him into prison, into a long succession of illicit romances, and almost into parliament. His campaigns for Irish independence won him a sentence of two months' hard labour from an English court, and he remained a close friend and adviser of the Egyptian nationalist Ahmed Arabi, a connection which gained him no friends at all in London society.

But his commitment to the Arab world was emotional as well as political. Soon after his return from Nejd, he bought himself a thirty-seven-acre park near Heliopolis in Egypt, Sheykh Obeyd — a gesture, he said, of his faith in Egyptian nationalism.

His love for Arabia lasted through his life. More than thirty years after the pilgrimage to Nejd, he wrote that the bedu were "a people... more moral than their neighbours, and free from all contemptible crime, whose public life was based not in word only, but in fact, on those three principles so much abused in Europe: Liberty, Equality, and Brotherhood."

His personal life, though, was if anything even more tempestuous than his public one. In 1906, finally worn down by her husband's unconcealed succession of lovers and mistresses, Lady Anne left him. She died in 1917, alone and reading sadly over her husband's old letters to her, and was buried within sight of the beloved park of Sheykh Obeyd.

Blunt himself struggled on, a sick and ageing eccentric, dressed in full Arab robes to receive Yeats, Pound and the other young poets of the day, who revered him as a master. Harry St John Philby and T E Lawrence were among his visitors: perhaps in the young explorers and adventurers, Blunt saw something of himself. In 1922, at the age of eighty-two, he died, a man who had touched a distant world, and never quite let go.

WAR IN THE DESERT

"My ride was long and dangerous, no part of the
machinery of the revolt, as barren of consequence as
it was unworthy of motive…"

– T E Lawrence

The rival houses of Saud and Rashid had been feuding for generations, and the power of the Ottoman Empire in Arabia was limping painfully towards its end. The early years of the twentieth century were years of warfare, which were eventually to set the foundations of the modern states of the Gulf — and for most of the explorers who ventured into the desert, travel and discovery were mere secondary considerations compared with the urgent need for military advantage.

One, though, seemed to ignore the gathering war clouds to mount a private expedition that was reminiscent of the Victorians in its idiosyncratic confidence and dash. Gertrude Bell was leaving Damascus for Hail in the centre of the Arabian peninsula in late 1913, just as Europe was stumbling towards conflict. At home in England, like the Blunts, she was a person of impeccable social standing, and here in the desert too, she expected to be treated with due deference and respect. At forty-four, she was struggling in the painful throes of a hopeless and potentially scandalous love affair.

The man she loved, Major Dick Doughty-Wylie, was a diplomat and highly-decorated soldier, and also the nephew of the great Charles Doughty — but he was also married. In a sense, perhaps, Gertrude Bell was running away from her heart when she planned her expedition to Hail — although the two continued to exchange occasional passionate letters until Doughty-Wylie was killed in the carnage of Gallipoli.

Certainly, his letters followed her to Arabia — and the determination with which she had turned her back on the affair was matched by the strength of purpose she showed on the journey. Both her femininity and her determination stood her in good stead: she had acquired a poise and confidence which desert Arabs respected.

She rode south from Damascus, accompanied by a small group of Arab guides, slipping past the attempts of British and Turkish officialdom to stop her on the way. As she approached Hail, after two months in the desert, she began to worry about her reception, which she expressed, like Lady Anne Blunt, in the understated way one might expect from a lady of her social class and background. "I hope the Hail people will be polite," she wrote, a trifle nervously. They were, even if her appearance and bearing must have astonished them.

Hail had developed something of a tradition of receiving unlikely European guests riding out of the desert: Palgrave had arrived there some fifty years earlier, and Doughty and the Blunts had followed, to receive their different greetings. But the Arab authorities had never seen or heard of anyone like Gertrude Bell. When they jibbed at cashing her a cheque for two hundred pounds — a massive sum in those days, particularly as they had no way of knowing whether her signature would be honoured — she announced abruptly that she would leave the next day.

The Emir himself was away on an expedition, and his brother Ibrahim was in charge in his place. It says something about Gertrude Bell's manner and force of character that the possible loss of his two hundred pounds paled into insignificance before the prospect of her outspoken displeasure. The money arrived ceremoniously that evening, carried by a palace slave, along with a pointed request that she should indeed leave Hail the next day.

But, having travelled this far, she had no intention of leaving the city until she had seen all she had read about in her studying of Palgrave's book. She would stay, she declared, until she had been conducted around Hail in a proper manner.

This was the city which Lady Anne Blunt had approached with a delicious trepidation as she considered the possibility of having her head lopped off at a whim. But Ibrahim's reaction to Gertrude Bell's presumption was courteous and diplomatic in the extreme. She was escorted around the town, marvelling at the 'noiseless slow footfall of the camel', whose measured tread provided Hail's only traffic, and not until the next day, honour duly satisfied on both sides, was she politely shown the gates of the city.

From there she travelled on to Baghdad, where, summoned back again from home after the outbreak of war, she spent the next few years as a British government official.

These were years of irresistible tides moving across Arabia. The century had begun with the recapture of Riyadh from the Rashidi by the House of Saud in an operation involving a journey across the Empty Quarter which more than matched anything either before or since for courage and hardihood. Forty men set out on camels from Kuwait, where the Saudis were in exile, and struggled south across the Empty Quarter. Unlike the European explorers in the desert, these men did not even pretend to be interested in geological observations or the gathering of specimens: instead, they carefully swept away their footprints as they rode, to avoid trackers, and travelled silently and at night, working their way around to approach and seize Riyadh in a surprise attack.

Where European travellers might aspire to cover fifteen miles in a day, these tribesmen lost themselves in the sands for fifty days before dashing in to approach the city from the south in a week-long trek which averaged over thirty miles a night — and after that, instead of resting, they mounted a determined and successful surprise attack. Dedicated and brave as adventurers like the Blunts or Burton, or even Gertrude Bell may have been, the comparison between their journeys and that of the Arab soldiers is one between amateurs and professionals, between dilettantes and hardened desert travellers.

The recapture of Riyadh in 1902 started a resurgence of Saudi power. One city after another fell, until by 1913, the Saudis held Boreyda and Aneyza as well as Riyadh, and the Ottoman empire had been driven out of Hasa. Against the remaining Ottomans were ranged not only the Saudis, but also the Sheriff of Mecca, and the Rashidi, in their reduced stronghold of Hail; an uneasy alliance, and one which the western powers, with a sharp eye for their own advantage, watched avidly.

When the British army captain William Shakespear set off for Riyadh in 1914 on a visit to ibn Saud — whom he had met while working as a diplomat in Kuwait — it was with the permission and keen interest of the British government. The journey took him two months: there were nights of bitter frost, and days of blazing sun as he crossed the deep red dunes of the Dahna desert, and after he reached the Saudi capital, he spent another two months travelling through Boreyda, Jof, and the Hejaz to Sinai.

It was a journey of nearly two thousand miles, with the camels weak from exhaustion and lack of food, and Shakespear himself rambling from sunstroke. But London's interest in his achievement was political rather than geographic: with the Ottoman Empire allied with Germany in the First World War, the British government saw great advantage for itself in Shakespear's friendship with ibn Saud — the more so as ibn Saud's Rashidi rivals were newly allied with Britain's Ottoman enemies.

It was barely six months after the triumphant end of his journey that Shakespear was killed in a desert skirmish with the Rashidi. His journey — and his death — ultimately achieved little, but they set the precedent for the complex of military and political motives that were to guide European involvement in Arabian travel over the next decades.

Shakespear's death at the hands of their allies gave the Turks the evidence they wanted of western — and non-Muslim —interference in

Arabia, and they exploited it with determination. But when they triumphantly displayed his pathetic pith helmet outside Medina, the real British involvement in the Arab struggle for independence had not even begun.

By 1915, war was already raging on one side of the world, imminent on another. In Europe, the great powers were locked into the miserable attrition of the First World War, while in Arabia, the tribes were beginning to shake themselves free of the last grasp of the Ottoman Empire. For years, the empire had been tottering — many of the soldiers Doughty had met, far from their homes, were not paid or even fed for months or years at a stretch — but once the Arab Revolt had started, the Turks poured men and equipment into the peninsula in a last, desperate attempt to regain their grip.

Ibn Saud withdrew into a wary neutrality, anxious of losing all that he had won already, but further west, in the Hejaz, the Hashemite Sheriff Hussain began the revolt that was ultimately to drive the Turks out of Damascus and most of their empire. Bertram Thomas, the diffident British civil servant who was to become the first westerner to cross the Empty Quarter, wrote later: "Here was a powder magazine within the Turkish territories ready to be fired by the war in which these politically-minded Arabs saw their chance of flinging off the Turkish yoke."

They seized that chance on June 5, 1916, and soon after the outbreak of their revolt the young English officer, Thomas Edward Lawrence — Lawrence of Arabia — was at the side of Hussain's commanders.

Lawrence's place in the story of exploration in the Arabian deserts is an equivocal one. He was a soldier and a diplomat rather than a traveller in the classic sense. He made no discoveries, and stayed for the most part on trails that were already well enough known. Much of his campaigning in any case was done north of the Empty Quarter, in Palestine, Jordan, and Syria; and yet he writes with sympathy, passion, and understanding of the Arab tribesmen with whom he travelled. It is impossible to ignore *Seven Pillars of Wisdom* as an incisive comment on the gulf between two cultures, a lament over the impossibility of bridging the gap, and a poetic tribute to the desert and its people.

Within a few months of the start of the revolt in June 1916, the Turks had been driven out of Mecca itself, and Sheriff Hussain's sons Feisal, Ali and Abdullah were leading attacks on Medina, the railway north, Taif, and the Red Sea port of Jeddah. A report back to London late that year from the British Arab Bureau based in Cairo observed: "The Arabs, without the assistance of any non-Arab troops, have secured their independence in the part of Arabia where lies the very heart and centre of their national and religious sentiment."

But their achievements were fragile: the Turkish garrison at Medina had proved too well-armed and determined to be dislodged, despite repeated attempts to cut its supply line through the railway, and it was clear that pressing the revolt forward would involve harrying the occupying Turks further north.

Lawrence was sent in initially simply to report back to Cairo on the prospects of the Arab forces; there was already concern at their unconventional and undisciplined mode of warfare, and at the way the various armies seemed to operate more or less independently of each other. One of his first reports seemed to confirm the staff officers' fears. "The forces actually mobilised are continually shifting," he wrote in a revealing description of the bedu at war. "A family will have a gun, and its sons will serve in turn, perhaps week by week, and go home for a change as often as replaced. Married men drop off occasionally to see their wives, or a whole clan gets tired, and takes a rest."

When he had been there a few months, he saw the Arab forces slightly differently. The indiscipline was still there, of course, and the lack of military single-mindedness, but now Lawrence revealed his fascination with the enthusiasm and dash of the Arab forces as they followed Hussain's son, Feisal. "Behind us, three banners of purple silk, with gold spikes, behind them three drummers playing a march, and behind them a wild bouncing mass of twelve hundred camels of the bodyguard, all packed as closely as they could move, the men in every variety of coloured clothes, and the camels nearly as brilliant in their trapping — and the whole crowd singing at the tops of their voices a war song in honour of Feisal and his family."

It was hardly the sort of warfare envisaged by the British officer class, and the reaction of the career soldiers, with their ideas of discipline and the primacy of military strategy, can be easily imagined. It was not, either, the sort of secretive guerrilla campaign that was later to rewrite the military textbooks the soldiers were studying. But what Lawrence quickly came to understand was that the war against the Turks would have to be a specifically Arab-style guerrilla campaign, with lightly-armed tribesmen sweeping suddenly out of the desert on an unprepared enemy.

Loyalty to the common purpose among the Arabs themselves was shifting and uncertain: the army was made up of tribesmen whose allegiance was first and foremost to their own family group. Bitter feuds had been abandoned for the period of the campaign, but there was no telling when they might suddenly flare up again. There was no hope of changing the traditions of the independent-minded Arab tribesmen, and little point in trying. Much better to work with the grain of the Arab character, Lawrence reasoned. "After all, it's an Arab war," he wrote back in one report. "The Arabs have the right to go their own way and run things as they please. We are only guests."

The official view of Lawrence himself at that stage was hardly enthusiastic in any way: in his senior officers' early reports of him, descriptions like 'amateur', 'off-hand and rude', 'untidy', and 'unmilitary' crop up with military regularity. "I look upon him as a bumptious young ass," one officer observed. It seems that Lawrence, like most of the individuals who fell under the spell of the desert, did not easily relate to authority or officialdom.

He, in turn, was less than enchanted with the strategy and priorities of his commanders. From very early on, he realised that the British had no genuine desire to welcome the independent Arab nation they had promised to see established after the war, and the knowledge of his own part in that duplicity ate at his soul. On one occasion, he sent back a message saying: "The situation is so interesting that I think I will fail to come back. I want to rub off my British habits and go off with Feisal for a bit. Amusing job, and all new country…"

Despite the disingenuously casual tone, the intelligence officer had apparently been seduced by the country and the culture in which he had immersed himself. Lawrence's adoption of Arab dress — unpopular with his fellow officers — was more than ostentation. As much as any of the peace-time travellers of the desert, he was overwhelmed with respect and affection for his travelling companions.

Arab traditions, though, brought Lawrence nightmares of their own, one in particular probably more terrible than anything any of the other travellers faced. As the army moved northwards, he was told one day that an Ageyl tribesman in its ranks had been shot dead by a Moroccan who was also serving Feisal. The other Ageyl were demanding instant justice — blood for blood — and would not be dissuaded. Knowing that the resultant tit-for-tat reprisals might tear the fragile inter-tribe alliances of the army apart, the only solution was that Lawrence himself, a stranger without family, and not subject to the laws of the blood-feud, should be the executioner.

The murderer cried and begged for mercy, but the traditions of desert justice were strict and unbending. With his hand already trembling from fever, Lawrence shot him three times, leaving him to be buried by the relatives of the Ageyl he had murdered. Honour was satisfied, but Lawrence never forgot the cries of the first man he had killed in the Arab Revolt.

Lawrence's regard for the Arab way of life can be seen in his adherence to their code of conduct. In another incident, he discovered that one of the Arabs had fallen from his camel and been left behind in the desert. On foot, he would never overtake the party, but the Ageyl tribesmen, to whom he was not related and who therefore owed him neither loyalty nor concern, were not prepared to turn round to look for him. As a Christian and a foreigner, Lawrence knew he would not be expected to take on the duty of finding the lost man, but even so, he turned his camel around and set off back down the line of men and baggage out into the desert. It was an act of some courage, because the hard ground meant that the party was leaving no tracks. Lawrence might find the lost man, and still be unable to rejoin the rest of the party: he, too, could face death in the desert sun.

"Not a long death," he mused later. "Even for the very strongest, a second day in summer was all — but very painful, for thirst was an active malady: a fear and a panic which tore at the brain and reduced the bravest man to a stumbling, babbling maniac in an hour or two; and then the sun killed him."

Lawrence knew well what he was risking. It was not for personal regard of the man himself — "a gap-toothed, grumbling fellow, skrimshank in all our marches, bad-tempered, suspicious, brutal, a man whose engagement I regretted" — and only partly because of his knowledge that being seen to accept Arab duties would give him credit among the others and help to make the journey a success. Lawrence, like Thesiger, wanted to live up to the ideal of the bedu tribesmen. But it was important that he should succeed, and not just for his own troubled self-esteem. He was relying at least partly on personal respect for himself to hold the group together in a hazardous attempt on the Turkish stronghold at Aqaba.

As the Arab army made its way north, capturing the coastal settlement of Wejh from the Turks en route, Lawrence had devised a strategy of his own for taking the port of Aqaba, crucial for keeping Feisal's forces supplied by allied ships once they reached the northern deserts. He proposed that rather than attack from the sea, running the gauntlet of the Turkish defensive positions, the Arabs should trek through the desert to sweep down onto Aqaba from the landward side.

No European force could hope to complete the six-hundred-mile journey through the sands that such a plan would involve. It was designed specifically to capitalise on the unique strengths of the bedu tribesmen, and even they would not be able to take artillery, machine guns, or equipment: the plan relied on mobility and surprise.

It relied, too, on Lawrence's own ability to complete six hundred agonising miles. "We marched on, over monotonous, glittering sand; and over those worse stretches, *giaan*, of polished mud, nearly as white and smooth as laid paper, and often whole miles square. They blazed back the sun into our faces with glassy vigour, so we rode with its light raining direct arrows on our heads, and its reflection glancing up from the ground through our inadequate eyelids.

"It was not a steady pressure, but a pain ebbing and flowing; at one time piling itself up and up till we nearly swooned; and then falling away coolly in a moment of false shadow like a black web crossing the retina: these gave us a moment's breathing space to store new capacity for suffering, like the struggles to the surface of a drowning man..."

But despite being so arduous — or perhaps because it was so arduous — the trek remained an Arab journey, rather than a military expedition. Lawrence and the other leading figures were expected to accept formal Arab hospitality as they ate each day, sharing their visits around the various tribes so as not to give offence. Like many other travellers, Lawrence was overwhelmed by the extent of bedu hospitality. Sheikh Auda bin Abu Tayi, the leader of the local tribes north of Wejh, became a close friend on the journey to Aqaba. He was known as a fierce fighter — he claimed to have torn out the heart of a dying enemy, and eaten it then and there — but he also had a far-flung reputation for open-handedness.

"His hospitality is sweeping... His generosity has reduced him to poverty, and devoured the profits of a hundred successful raids," Lawrence wrote later. Other lesser chiefs could only seek to emulate him, though preferably, presumably, not necessarily to the extent of reducing themselves to penury.

Coffee, as ever, was an important ritual on the march. A slave would pour a few drops from one of the traditional beaked copper pots into one of three or four small white cups; when these were empty, they would be returned, and passed on to the next guests, and so on until all fifty or so had been served. Then the coffee would go round again, and then again, getting stronger and stronger as the pot poured deeper and deeper from the brew.

Then the meal itself would be served. The rice and meat, piled on a five-foot copper tray, would be carried in by two men. Two or three sheep, jointed and piled on the rice, made up the main course, their boiled heads forming an appetising centrepiece: "The jaws gaped emptily upward, pulled open to show the hollow throat with the tongue, still pink, clinging to the lower teeth; and the long incisors quietly crowned the pile, very prominent above the nostrils' pricking hair and the lips which sneered away blackly from them," wrote Lawrence. Gravy was poured over this by teams of helpers, and finally the whole livers were placed on the very top of the pile.

There was a certain reluctance to eat — feigned out of politeness by the Arabs, but increasingly genuine for Lawrence, who was suffering from a growing but understandable fastidiousness — but eventually twenty or so of the guests would encircle the dish, sink down on one knee, and dip in with their right hands, sleeves rolled back to the elbow. The host would stand by, encouraging them to take more. The guests themselves said little: conversation, it seemed, might insult the quality of the meal. When they had finished, the next group would come for their turn at the dish, until the gnawed bones and a few grains of greasy rice were left for the children to fight over.

There was more to trouble Lawrence than the constant feasting. He was well aware that the British promises of independence to the Arabs were bogus, even though he had no precise knowledge of the detailed bargain between French and English officials (the Sykes-Picot Agreement), which divided up the Middle East into spheres of influence. His part in recruiting Arabs to fight the Turks meant deceiving them about their prospects once the war was over; again and again, troubled by rumours of British duplicity, they would ask him for his personal assurances. "I was continually and bitterly ashamed," he wrote later. "It was evident from the beginning that if we won the war, these promises would be dead paper, and had I been an honest adviser of the Arabs, I would have advised them to go home and not risk their lives fighting for such stuff."

It was in that frame of mind that he set off north on his own, away from the main body of the army. Ostensibly, he was mounting a reconnaissance expedition, but the message he left in his notebook shows the way he was thinking. "I've decided to go off alone to Damascus, hoping to get killed on the way… We are calling them to fight for us on a lie, and I can't stand it."

But he survived. He travelled for thirteen days, a distance of some three hundred miles, leading raids against the Turks, meeting Arab nationalist leaders, and dissuading them from mounting any premature uprising. At the end of his journey, he found the recruitment complete, and Feisal's army several thousand strong and ready to move against Aqaba.

The main clash of the campaign came before they reached Maan, which guarded the approach down Wadi Itm to Aqaba. They surprised a Turkish battalion guarding one of the outlying passes, and some unguarded words of Lawrence's roused Sheikh Auda bin Abu Tayi to fury. Now the well-known host and man of generosity showed the other side of his character. "You shoot a lot and hit little," Lawrence mocked him. To prove the Englishman wrong, the elderly bedu mounted a savage charge of horse and camel against the unfortunate Turks.

"We kicked our camels furiously to the edge, to see our fifty horsemen coming down the last slope into the main valley, like a runaway, at full gallop, shooting from the saddle," he wrote. "We plunged our camels madly over the hill, and down towards the head of the fleeing enemy. The slope was not too steep for a camel-gallop, but steep enough to make their pace terrific, and their course uncontrollable… A charge of ridden camels going nearly thirty miles an hour was irresistible."

Lawrence's own part in the skirmish was less than distinguished — he was thrown semi-conscious into the sand when he accidentally shot his own camel in the back of the head and killed it — but the outcome of the charge was overwhelming victory for the Arabs.

Maan itself was lightly defended, but the decision was to pass it by, and head straight down Wadi Itm for Aqaba. Almost all the Turkish defences had been prepared to resist attack from the sea, and many that were set up in the valley itself had been evacuated. The Arab force sweeping down behind them threw the Turks into a panic, and there was hardly any opposition to the advance.

But for Lawrence, there was still not only hard desert campaigning ahead, but also bitter political argument about the future of the Arab state which had been promised. The capture of Aqaba in July 1917 was the end only of one campaign in a war that was to see Feisal and his forces in Damascus just over a year later — and soon after that, embroiled in the machinations of Anglo-French Middle East policy.

As he was not like other travellers in the desert, so his motives were different. To contribute to winning Britain's war, of course, and in the conflict between that and the ambitions of his Arab friends lay the roots of much of the guilt that tortured him. But there was more than that. "I meant to make a new nation, to restore a lost influence, to give twenty millions of Semites the foundation on which to build an inspired dream-palace of their national thoughts," he wrote later, in *Seven Pillars of Wisdom*. Instead of the glory that might accompany such a noble dream, he found nothing but constant shame in the political manoeuvrings of a determined imperial power.

More than any of the other travellers, though, he came to identify with the Arabs — he, after all, was travelling as part of a genuine Arab expedition, rather than in a European-led adventure — and more than any of the others, he came to appreciate the impossibility of being one of them.

His predecessors had written about the almost mystical feeling of being outside their own bodies, of looking down on themselves from a distance, when heat and weariness began to make them suffer. Lawrence took that suffering further, and saw in the delusion an image of the way he had left behind one culture, and failed to find another. "Sometimes these two selves would converse in the void; and then madness was very near, as I believe it would be near the man who could see things through the veils at once of two customs, two educations, two environments."

At the end of 1917, a British diplomat arrived in Arabia on a fresh mission to reach ibn Saud in Riyadh. The British, with Lawrence's aid, were already arming the Sheriff of Mecca, and encouraging him in his revolt against the Turkish forces: now they wanted ibn Saud to renew his campaign against the Turks' Arab allies in Hail.

Harry St John Philby later claimed to have been the first socialist in the Indian Civil Service, but his travels in Arabia made him an even more singular figure. The fascination of the desert, of Arab culture, Arab religion, and of ibn Saud himself, gripped him for the rest of his life, and he became one of the greatest of the explorers to conquer the Empty Quarter.

According to his own account, the determination to become the first European to cross the sands dated almost from his arrival at the port of Uqayr, but it was to be another fifteen years before he was to have his chance. On this first visit, he had a diplomatic brief to carry out for his government, although he found an imaginative way to transform the mission itself into a full-scale desert expedition.

Along with the gloriously-named Lt-Col Cunliffe-Owen, another of the British government's orientalists, and his batman, he set off in his khaki uniform, pith helmet and leather boots on the three-day trek to Hofuf, from where they were to begin the journey across the Dahna Desert to Riyadh. Fifty years before, William Gifford Palgrave had struggled for five days in the red sands of the Dahna: Philby, travelling in the opposite direction, curtly wrote off its terrors as "grossly exaggerated".

The little expedition — dressed by now in Arab clothes which had been provided for them by the governor of Hofuf — was welcomed into Riyadh at the end of their journey by ibn Saud's father. But it was with ibn Saud himself, the man whom he was later to call 'the Arabian Caesar', and 'my hero since the first days of our easy friendship' that Philby spent most of his time in the city.

The diplomacy was not easy. Ibn Saud contrasted the vast supplies and modern weapons being sent to the Sheriff of Mecca with the few chests of equipment that had been supplied to his own sparsely-equipped forces. Even worse, the Sheriff was refusing to allow a second British mission to Riyadh permission to cross the Hejaz because, he claimed, the country to the east was wild and unclaimed — a deliberate attempt, said ibn Saud, to challenge his rule of the territory.

Philby's response was immediate: he would travel west across the desert with an escort of ibn Saud's men, to bring the British expedition back with him. Everyone, Philby may have reasoned sagely, would be happy: the expedition would reach its objective, ibn Saud would demonstrate his control of the territory, and he, Philby, would have the chance of becoming the first European to make the east to west crossing of the Peninsula for nearly a hundred years. "I should confess, perhaps, that my motives in making that proposal were of a mixed character, and not wholly based on the requirements of the situation, but that is a trifle…" he wrote later.

His two companions, despairing of any diplomatic success with ibn Saud, had already left for the Gulf and so, without giving his government time to object — their satisfaction, he might have guessed, would be tempered by dismay at the diplomatic row his journey would cause in Mecca — Philby departed with his small escort.

They set out, like most travellers, on the old Haj road, past the ruins of Diriyyah, which had been laid waste by the Turks a century before, and

then on, over the rocky landscape towards the rolling sand dunes of the
Nafud desert — the same desert in which Palgrave had struggled
through 'suffocating sand pits', and in which the Blunts had feared
they might end their journey in disaster. Philby was luckier: there was
rain, and even herds of gazelle in the Nafud, and further on, on the
way to Qusariyah, abundant supplies of game. From there, they
struggled for five days to make their way across the harsh central
Arabian highlands, Philby's mind always half on the journey itself and
half on the diplomatic bombshell he was about to drop.

In the sands, establishing ibn Saud's authority as he had promised,
he and his companions drew the King's mark with their sticks. The
lightest wind might blow it away — but for even a few tribesmen to see
it would be enough, in a country where news travelled as swiftly as it
did in Arabia, to put about the word that ibn Saud's arm stretched far
beyond the mountains, as he had claimed.

It was Christmas Day when the little group finally rode into Taif
after sixteen days' hard travelling. There was no-one to greet them, but
he had proved that it was possible to travel right across central Arabia
with ibn Saud's *laissez-passer*.

Word of the journey soon reached the ears of Sheriff Hussain, as ibn
Saud had intended — and, again as ibn Saud had intended, he was
furious. His rival had established his credentials as ruler of vast
stretches of Arabia, an outcome that angered his supporters in London
— Philby's Foreign Office masters — almost as much as it did the
Sheriff himself. Philby himself, characteristically, was delighted.

The Great War, like Philby's journey, settled little in Arabia: the
Ottoman Empire, of course, was dealt its death-blow, but it was 1924
before ibn Saud effectively controlled the Hejaz and what had been the
Rashidi stronghold of Hail. Philby, meanwhile, was chafing and
grumbling as Chief Political Adviser in the newly-created state of
Trans-Jordan — and, incidentally, making the acquaintance of the quiet,
scholarly Bertram Thomas.

Philby had travelled around the fringes of the Empty Quarter towards the end of the war, but when he finally returned to Arabia and his hero, ibn Saud, in the mid-Twenties, it was with a single, burning ambition: he wanted to be the first European to conquer the Empty Quarter. His first attempt in 1924 ended in failure before it had even begun, partly because of the fighting that was still raging between the tribes, and partly because of a crippling attack of dysentery. Philby had returned to make his home on the Red Sea coast of Arabia, but his journey had to be postponed. He was, he said, "a sick and disappointed man".

He had seven more years' wait and many more disappointments in store; and all the time, Bertram Thomas was quietly working towards the same goal.

SECRET DREAMS

"He is crazed with the spell of far Arabia,
They have stolen his wits away."

– Walter de la Mare, 'Arabia',
from the envoi to *Arabia Felix*.

Arab travellers early in this century formed an exclusive little group, turning to each other for support and understanding. T E Lawrence, who claimed barely to include himself in the list of the great Arabists, wrote in the foreword to Thomas's book, *Arabia Felix*:

"In my day, there were real Arabian veterans. Upon each return from the East, I would repair to Doughty, a looming giant, headed and bearded like some renaissance Isaiah. Doughty seemed a past world in himself; and after him, I would visit Wilfrid Blunt...

"Doughty's voice was a caress, his nature sweetness. Blunt was a fire yet flickering over the ashes of old fury." Doughty's nature, presumably, had sweetened with time.

But it was the journey of the softly-spoken Thomas which all the travellers who came after him acknowledged as among the greatest. From Philby's "Damn and blast Thomas" to Lawrence's more respectful assessment of the journey as "the finest thing in Arabian exploration", or to Wilfred Thesiger's regret that he never had the chance to tell him how much he owed him, the men who had known the desert paid their own tributes to the first European to conquer the Empty Quarter.

Even Philby, ungenerous as he was in his initial reaction, softened eventually. "His exploit was greeted with worldwide admiration, and learned societies hastened to honour him with their highest awards," he wrote twenty years later, after Thomas's death.

And yet Thomas was by far the most unlikely of the desert explorers. Educated at a West Country village school, and working for the Post Office at the age of sixteen, he seemed cut out for an unexceptionable life in a quiet office somewhere. And then came the First World War.

He joined the army, and after a spell in Belgium, he was posted to Mesopotamia. That, if anywhere, was where he was seized by 'the spell of far Arabia': two more years in the army were followed by four in the Government's Political Department, and then by a career as adviser to various Arab administrations.

Still, perhaps, he seemed to be the archetypal civil servant and bureaucrat — but all the time, he was studiously gathering an encyclopaedic knowledge of the Arabic language and of Arab customs. From Mesopotamia, he travelled to Muscat in 1924 to become financial adviser and later Prime Minister to the Sultan; and from Muscat, six years later, he eventually set out on the famous journey that was to take him across the Empty Quarter.

Less than a year before that, Lawrence had declared that only an airship could do it — but in 1930, Thomas left Muscat for his annual leave. Most Europeans took their time off in the heat of the summer, travelling to India to avoid the sun. Thomas, though, preferred to stay at his desk, husbanding his time off for the winter and his desert explorations.

By 1930, he had already made two major expeditions — a six hundred mile camel journey through southern Oman, and another two hundred miles north of Dhofar. With the exactitude of the professional administrator, he had been making his preparations for the climactic trek across the sands. "The virgin Rub Al Khali, the Great Southern Desert!" he wrote later. "To have laboured in Arabia is to have tasted inevitably of her seduction, and six years ago, when I left the administration of Transjordan for the Court of Muscat and Oman, I already cherished secret dreams..."

Secret they remained until the very last minute. Seeking permission from his superiors, he knew, would mean courting the risk of refusal — and so he left Muscat quietly, by night, on board a British oil-tanker which later transferred him to a passing dhow to land him at Salalah. A Rashidi tribesman named Sahail had agreed to meet him there, to lead him into the Empty Quarter — but, with tribal warfare raging in the region, his guide failed to keep the appointment. "The door to the sands seemed bolted and barred," Thomas wrote — but then, by chance, he met two other Rashidi, Khuwaitim and Ma'yuf. They agreed to carry back his message to their leader at his camp in the desert: Thomas would pay well if guides would escort him into the sands.

Possibly, after thirty or forty days, they would return with men and camels; possibly he would never see them again. It was a thin thread on which to hang his hopes of achieving his ambition.

As they left, he stopped one of the Rashidi. "'Here, Khuwaitim,' I said, 'You have no rifle. Take this one — it is a small present for you.'

"'What,' came the reply, as he took it from my hand and examined it critically. 'You are not going to give me any ammunition with it?'"

Thomas puzzled afterwards as to whether that exchange was simply an example of bedu greed and ingratitude, and decided eventually that it was more fatalism than either. It was the will of Allah that he should hand over his rifle, and so, from the bedu viewpoint, there was no call for gratitude. It's possible too, of course, that Khuwaitim saw the incident for what it was — an attempt to persuade him to support Thomas's endeavour, rather than a free-hearted gift. Gratitude might have been an appropriate and civil response by European standards, but it might not have been a particularly honest one.

While he waited in Salalah, Thomas had plenty to occupy his time. He had a pair of calipers with him, with which to measure the precise dimensions of the skulls of local people, in an effort to decide whether the inhabitants of South Arabia were a single, homogeneous racial group. His thirst for scientific knowledge seems sometimes to have blinded him to propriety, and even to ordinary human decency. He had hoped, he says, to unearth and send home actual human skulls for study, but he discovered, ruefully, that "the dangers of offending religious susceptibilities in Arabia were great" — as great, perhaps, as they might have been in England, had some eccentric Arab traveller started digging up a quiet country churchyard in order to restock his collection of human remains.

Along with the many other qualities they inherited from the Victorians, the explorers of the twentieth century seem to have had an overweening confidence in their own scientific endeavour — and a corresponding tendency to consider the people among whom they moved as little more than exhibits in the great human museum. The people themselves, frustratingly, seemed not to fall in with that view — and even when Thomas had realised he would have to settle for measurements of living skulls rather than collections of dead ones, he found a distinct unwillingness among the locals to subject themselves to examination at the points of his calipers.

In the desert, he suggested with some insight, he might have been unwilling to press his requests in case they met with a dagger in the ribs for answer: here in Dhofar, he restricted himself to examinations of friends, prisoners, and warders. Even so, he seems to have shown a marked lack of tact. "Are you quite sure you are pure-bred?" he asked a Somali police officer, whose skull inconsiderately failed to meet the criteria he thought it should. Not only was the question astonishingly ill-mannered, even for a colonial administrator — it also shows a significant naivete in the gathering of scientific data. It would be an unusual person who could swear to being entirely 'pure-bred', whatever that may mean.

He had all the self-confidence of an imperial civil servant. One of the subjects of his studies, for instance, told him contemptuously that farming and fishing were no work for a man — that wealth should be gathered by force of arms. "Fighting is all very well when the time for it comes," Thomas replied ponderously. "But how do you think we English became strong if it was not by work? How do you think we get our ships and our rifles?"

The young Arab was not convinced. He was presumably too kind to ask the representative of a race that had spread its power over half the world how precisely they used those rifles and those warships in fishing or in tilling the ground. But Thomas's studies passed the time — and if they did no good, then the fact that he survived his intrusive and occasionally offensive questioning without actually being assaulted suggests they probably did little harm either.

After two months' waiting, though, neither his anthropological studies nor a quickly-arranged expedition into the Qara Mountains could keep him in Salalah any longer. The two Rashidi tribesmen who had promised to bring their sheikh to him had not reappeared, and the ship that was to take him back to Muscat was waiting off the coast. On the next day, he would have to return to his official duties, and the long-dreamed-of exploration of the Empty Quarter would have to be postponed.

It was almost literally at the eleventh hour, then, that word finally came: the two bedu had arrived back in Salalah, with their sheikh and his companions waiting outside the town. Thomas decided to send the gunboat away: he would return to Muscat, he said — with considerable understatement, since his projected journey involved hundreds of miles across the desert in entirely the wrong direction — "by another way".

His plans, clearly, were fairly fluid. When he met Sheikh Salih bin Kalut, the Rashidi chief who was to lead him on the first stages of his journey, the sheikh asked him: "But at what place do you want to come out?"

"Wherever it is possible," Thomas replied. "Riyadh, Bahrain, Abu Dhabi!"

"Impossible, sahib," he said emphatically.

The Rashidi, he explained, could take Thomas into their own country around the southern sands, and bring him back again, despite the state of tribal warfare that existed ("and God preserve us from the Saar!") — but they dared not venture into the grazing lands of another tribe without a *rabia* from that tribe — a companion who would stand as his guarantor.

It was the same system the Blunts had found a century before: with a companion from among the people who inhabited the area, or from another friendly tribe, the traveller might be safe from attack. Without one, he and the rest of his party would be likely to be killed by the first Arabs they met in the desert.

It was some time before Salih agreed to help: but eventually, with the offer of generous payment in his mind, he promised to do his best to find Thomas a *rabia* from among the Murri, the tribe who controlled the central deserts. He left Dhofar with an escort of forty Rashidi. That, he reckoned, was the minimum safe number, even with the protection of a *rabia* — and even that might not be enough, when rumours leaked out of the 3,000 silver dollars he was carrying to pay his tribesmen. That sort of booty would make the party a tempting target for raiding parties that might number as many as three hundred men.

With his Arab companions, he took fifteen pack animals, laden with rations of butter, rice, dates, and flour. The plan was to make the journey in four relays, with camels and men changing at watering holes on the route — and the aim was nothing less than to complete the first recorded crossing of the Empty Quarter.

The reason for his journey, he told his companions, was simply a love of travel and the pursuit of knowledge — mapping the interior, studying its geology and formation, cataloguing the plants and animals of the desert. It was a similar list to that put forward by most of his predecessors, and it hid a similar, unspoken, ambition — the desire to pit himself against the harshest conditions the world could offer.

The first hurdle, though, was simply to get the party on its way. "The departure of the bedu is ever sluggish; his thoughts are with his camel under its strange and heavy load; then he himself has forgotten something he wanted from the bazaar, which he sees but once in many moons, and he hands his camel over to a neighbour's charge and goes back to dally there for an hour or more..."

Thomas was learning early, as Lawrence had learned on his military expeditions, that it was as well to travel with the Arabs on their own terms, or not to set out at all.

Only five miles out of Salalah, the Arabs spotted some thorn bushes at which their camels might eat, and within a few moments, the first day's march had ended. Only then, with the expedition actually begun, did the real preparations start to take place, with the tribesmen stitching up sacks of hay for use as pack saddles, oiling their all-important water skins, cutting themselves riding canes, and even stitching an impromptu leather patch on the injured foot of one of the camels, in the same way that Philby saw on his journey. By seven the next morning, though, they were on their way — although this time, too, they travelled only for a couple of hours before stopping to inspect the famous Ghaur Fazl, a twenty-foot-wide hole in the grassy foothills.

Thomas investigated it just as travellers must have done for centuries — by the simple expedient of dropping a small stone into it. It took a couple of seconds to reach the bottom, suggesting that the hole must be around two hundred feet deep.

A mile further into the limestone hills was another hole in the rocks — the huge Cave of Sahour this time, a gaping hole about one hundred feet wide by forty feet high in the rock face. The entire group was persuaded to ignore the possibility of djinns and evil spirits, and to slither feet first into a small hole at the back of the cave, which led them into a large underground chamber, with stalagmites, stalactites, and walls of dazzling white crystalline rock. The cave system, according to reports, extended back miles into the mountain: Thomas, though, was anxious to make a proper start on his journey.

They made their way from Sahour up steeply wooded mountain slopes, then across the gently undulating meadow terrain that followed, at around 1,300 feet. Even though they seemed far from Salalah, there was a reminder along the way that the Sultan still enforced the law with vigour in these remote parts — an old man of the Qara tribe, who had been found guilty of theft years before, and now nursed a withered stump instead of a hand. "The appointed slave at the fort had made a good job of it with one blow of the axe," Thomas noted meticulously, and without much apparent sympathy.

Slowly and laboriously, his party picked its way up into the hills, through more thick woods and shrubland, until they stood at the summit of the Qara Mountains. Behind them, 3,000 feet below, was a last glimpse of the Indian Ocean, and in front, the prospect of pale sandstone hills, frankincense groves, and finally, the barren sands of the desert.

At each campsite, as they made their way towards Shis'r, they checked for signs of enemies or robbers who might be tracking them. For a hundred miles, his companions told him, any party they might meet was a potential adversary.

Dropping down on the northern side of the mountains, through the soft sand of the wadi beds, Thomas had his first glimpse of the frankincense trees on which the ancient prosperity of the region had depended, going through groves of the withered, bush-like trees for about an hour as the party descended the hillside. It sounds an unimpressive plant on which to base an entire economy. "In appearance, it is a young sapling, having almost no central trunk, but from near the ground there springs out a clump of branches which grow to a camel's height and more, with ash-coloured bark, and tiny crumpled leaves," Thomas wrote.

As they passed through the frankincense groves, some twenty miles from the sea, they were leaving behind the last permanent human settlements they were to find. From here on, the people they met would be nomads, not farmers — and every one would be a potential enemy.

From here on, too, there would be no more limestone mountains. There stretched in front of them six days of walking over a stony sandstone steppe, the home of tribes such as the Bait Kathir, the Mahra, and the Bait ash Shaikh — and after that, the apparently limitless sands of the Empty Quarter itself.

At last Thomas felt that the journey had really begun — and he began, too, to make the acquaintance of his travelling companions. "It was a joy to be in the saddle again, and a joy to have left the busy, humdrum world of Dhofar behind for these wide, clean spaces," he wrote. "I missed the rousing camel chanties of the march in Oman... still, they were merry enough conversationalists, even if their subjects were limited to camels, rifles, and women..."

The next water-hole at Shis'r lay four days' journey ahead, and so the first priority was to pause at Hanun to let the camels drink, and to fill their own water-skins. Thomas had been promised that the water of Hanun would be sweet and good to drink, but he was to discover what his predecessors had found out as well — that terms like 'sweet' and 'brackish' have their own meaning in the desert. What on earth, he wondered as he gingerly washed the water around his mouth, would the water they described as brackish taste like?

But his fastidiousness wasn't enough to deflect him from the serious business of collecting specimens to take home with him. On one occasion, he shot an oryx, carefully preserving the skin for the experts at the museum; he took careful drawings of little groups of stones arranged like tripods which he came across along the way — "probably graves", he noted, and added regretfully that he had only been able to carry off one single stone, marked with an engraving which seemed to represent a camel. Once again, the enthusiasm of a Victorian explorer seems to be mixed up with the ethics of a grave-robber: but then, Thomas was travelling in a less sensitive age.

The party split up soon after it left Hanun, with Salih, the Rashidi chief who had first agreed to help him, hurrying ahead to spy out the route with a single companion and no baggage camels to slow him down. With him, he had some meagre rations of flour and dates, along with a robe as a gift for the Murri sheikh he hoped to persuade to take over the job of guiding the party after it reached Dhahiya, the water-hole where he intended to rejoin them. Thomas and the main party, meanwhile, set off north-west across a series of low hills and ridges, many of the camels carrying large bundles of palm fronds which had been gathered by the Arabs to present to their womenfolk back in the camp. The women would weave the fronds into basins, while the men would use them to make rope and sacking. Either way, they were too valuable a commodity for a people used to life in the barrenness of the desert to leave behind.

Thomas was already having problems with his scientific equipment. He was carrying three chronometers, two aneroid barometers, and a wet and dry bulb thermometer, and he found that sand kept getting into them as he struggled to manipulate them in the darkness. In addition, he found that the Pole Star was so close to the horizon that it was difficult to take an accurate reading with his sextant.

Most trying of all, though, was the problem of secrecy. He was anxious not to be spotted taking his readings, in case the tribesmen with him suspected him of casting magic spells with the stars — and keeping the operation secret simply added to his problems. In fact, the Arabs were much too preoccupied with their camels to worry about the strange preoccupations of their European companion. Care for the animals on which they relied far outweighed every other aspect of the journey — something which Thomas simply had to adapt to. "The traveller in the desert soon discovers that the welfare of the camel is the supreme consideration... Fodder is almost more important than water, for the camel can carry a load for a week or more without water, but food is a daily want," he wrote. "The European accustomed to a programme, a time to start, a time to halt, a time to eat, and an expectation of a certain average daily mileage, gets a rude shock."

Frequently, if the camels came upon good fodder, the day's journey would be cut short so that they could eat. Three hours was all they managed one day, four or five another: if the camels failed to find enough food to keep them going, then the men would die. It was as simple as that.

As they struggled on towards Shis'r — only too well aware that this was only a prelude to the real journey across the sands — they eventually left behind the last slight ridges to start across the flat, featureless, sandy plain of the Nej'd Desert.

Here and there, relieving the boredom, were little nests of fossilised oysters, still lying where they had done for thousands of years, even though the surrounding area had changed from ocean bed to the field of flint and rubble that now stretched to the horizon on all sides. "Not a vestige of vegetation," Thomas noted tersely — the only movement was the occasional whirling 'sand-devils', spinning columns of sand, which brought refreshing gusts of wind in their train. For the next two days, they plodded steadily on across the hard, sandy floor towards Shis'r and the promise of water.

With water, though, came the threat of danger. They approached the rocky knoll which stood above the little spring with care, in case other tribesmen were already in possession — a common precaution, in hostile country. It was usual, too, Thomas was told, for travellers to fill in a water-hole when they had used it, so that any pursuers would have to delay while they dug it out — but here at Shis'r, the wind did the job itself. In a couple of days, the sand covered the entrance to the precious water-hole.

It was a site that Ranulph Fiennes was to visit more than fifty years later — a wide, stoneless plain, surrounding a rocky outcrop. On top of the rock were what seemed to be the ruins of an ancient fort — and underneath it, about fifty feet deep at the back of a cave, was the spring. The gap in the rocky floor was barely big enough to squeeze a human arm into it, and at the bottom, the spring was a mere trickle. The only way to water the camels was with small leather buckets carefully pulled up by hand. It took hours to do, with guards keeping a constant watch for approaching strangers, but between the triumph of what they had achieved and the magnitude of the challenge that lay ahead, the hardship hardly mattered. The triumph was that the little party had crossed the Nej'd: the challenge, that the sands of the Empty Quarter were barely a day's journey away.

Before them, though, still lay a hundred miles or more of dangerous marches — probably the most difficult and perilous part of their journey. It was not just the barren landscape that threatened their survival, but the undoubted hostility of the tribes which they might encounter. Although it was a waterless no-man's land that they were setting out to cross, it was also criss-crossed with trails from one water-hole to another — trails, Thomas's companions pointed out, that would be used only by raiders bent on plunder and casual murder.

Their warnings were dire — but their preparations for attack seem to have been rudimentary to say the least. Perhaps, as Thomas supposed, it was the natural fatalism of the desert Arabs — but there is at least a suspicion that his guides, like those of the Blunts and others before him, might have been taking some pleasure in building up the dangers of the trail for the benefit of their European companion.

"My party betrayed by word, look, and act that they were on tenterhooks, and whenever my camel bore me ahead of them, or lagged behind, someone was soon beside me to remind me that we were in dangerous country — yet on making camp, never were there dispositions made so far as I could see for making an attack or escaping from one," he wrote.

On one occasion later in the march, the cry of a wolf in the dark of the night sparked off fears that a raid was imminent, and then Thomas saw the Arabs' reaction. The guides, *rabia*, ran out into the open, shouting their names and those of their tribes, so that any attackers would know that the party had at least some measure of protection. It was a procedure that relied entirely on trust on each side and it was not, Thomas observed with a very western wonder, apparently ever abused.

Across the Desert, *Giulio Rosati. The Arabs' legendary fascination with horse-breeding was one of the reasons for the Blunts' journey through Arabia. (Mathaf Gallery)*

Portrait of Wilfrid Scawen Blunt. A life-long friend to the Arabs, even into old age he would affect Arab dress and customs both as a mark of respect, and as a way of shocking unwary visitors. (Bodleian Library)

Lady Anne Blunt, an English aristocrat and devotee of the exotic life of the Orient. (Bodleian Library)

Ghazu at the Wadi Sirhan. *Lady Anne's own view of the attack upon the little party: "Resistance seemed to me useless, and I shouted to the nearest horseman, 'Ana dahilak' (I am under your protection), the usual form of surrender…" (Bodleian Library)*

A Halt in the Desert, *J A Benwell, 1865. The Victorians' view of romance and exotic comforts of life in the desert often bore very little relation to reality. (Mathaf Gallery)*

Above: The Arabs who had no choice but to travel through the desert could never understand why Doughty chose to do so. And he never told them. (ADCO)

Right: "Everything that is good about the Arabs has come from the desert. The only society in which I've found nobility is that of the bedu," Wilfred Thesiger. (ADCO)

Above: Gertrude Lowthian Bell. (Royal Geographical Society, London)

Above left: Harry St John Philby in his Mecca garden. (Royal Geographical Society, London)

Left: Philby escorted in Iidda, Hejaz, Arabia. (Royal Geographical Society, London)

Overleaf: The Attack, *Eugene Girardet, 1894. The widespread fighting of the early twentieth century was a continuation of tribal warfare which had been going on for generations. (Mathaf Gallery)*

Eugène Girardet 94

Wilfred Thesiger, the only European to cross the sands twice. "All my past had been but a prelude for the five years that lay before me," he wrote in Arabian Sands. *(Wilfred Thesiger)*

Bin Kabina and bin Ghabaisha, Thesiger's travelling companions for his journeys across the Empty Quarter. He never, he said, felt lonely in the desert, nor anywhere among Arabs. (Wilfred Thesiger)

Overleaf: Thesiger's party crossing the Empty Quarter, December 1946. (Wilfred Thesiger)

Ranulph Fiennes with the Sultan's Armed Forces, Oman, 1968. (Royal Geographical Society, London)

Ranulph Fiennes removing an anti-tank mine with care, due to the possibility of a grenade underneath. (Royal Geographical Society, London)

So perhaps the Arabs were, in fact, making their preparations for dealing with attackers without Thomas being aware of it; perhaps they simply felt a stoic acceptance of whatever fate had in store for them; but perhaps, too, they enjoyed the effect that their warnings of the undoubted dangers must have had on Thomas. They may also, of course, have reasoned that the more dangerous the journey seemed, the more profitable it might be later in terms of the Maria Theresa dollars he was carrying.

For five days they plodded steadily westward into the afternoon sun, skirting the southern fringe of the great sands with their eyes constantly scanning the horizon for the first sign of a possible attack. One of the party would be sent ahead to spy out the land from a vantage point and see that it was clear of raiders, before the others trooped past silently below. And yet, it was a strangely inconsistent caution: on spotting good grazing for the camels, the wary spy would suddenly leap in the air, shouting and waving his headcloth to attract attention, all thought of discretion and possible attack gone.

Beyond Fasad, the plain became stony and undulating. There was a brief pause at Mitan and then, on Christmas Eve, they headed into the 'red mountains of sand' of the great dune country. This was the terrain for which they had been preparing themselves and saving their camels. Now, Thomas could see the reason for the almost obsessive care the Arabs took of their animals.

For hours at a time, they would toil up towering dunes and then struggle down the other side. "Our camels, wretched beasts, climbed arduously up to knife edge summits, and slithered knee-deep down precipitous slopes. Here and there, we turned back for very fear, and tried a better way..." The men were floundering too, sinking ankle-deep into the soft sand at every step. It would, said Thomas with some satisfaction, have been impassable for horses or cars. "But our toil had its compensations. There were moments when we came suddenly on a picture of sublime grandeur, immense and noble plastic architecture, an exquisite purity of colour, old rose-red under a cloudless sky and brilliant light."

At the end of the day, they reached the wide valley of Khor Dhahiya, where they had arranged to rendezvous with Salih. Three hundred feet below them was the water-hole — but, even though they were a day late in arriving, there was no sign of Salih.

For the Muslim Arabs, there was, however, cause enough for celebration because they and their weary camels could rest: and for Thomas himself, the disappointment of not finding Salih was not allowed to interfere with the festivity of Christmas dinner. Desiccated soup and a tin of baked beans, after a strenuous nine-hour march without solid food, apparently constituted a suitably festive meal.

A couple of days later, the Arabs were able to return the compliment by providing him with a dish of boiled camel meat — although the Arabs took immense care of their camels, they were entirely unsentimental about them if they became lame or ill on the march. The freshly-cooked meat was a rare treat for them, but less so for Thomas. "I will record my own view that camel flesh is very tough and stringy, and that boiled, as it has to be, in brackish water and without fat, it is a weariness both to the palate and the digestion," he said. Maybe, of course, the finest English lamb would not have been improved in either tenderness or taste by a forced march across the dunes, followed by a marinade of desert water — but there was worse to come.

With the remains of the camel meat prepared to dry like strips of biltong on the saddles, the final delicacy was the yellow liquid that lay in the unfortunate beast's stomach. "'It is delicious,' they said, as each in turn went down on hands and knees, setting it to his lips to drink his fill..." Perhaps, to the delicate palate of a European civil servant, desiccated soup and baked beans might have seemed in comparison like a fairly luxurious repast.

It was in the soft sand around the campsite that they eventually found traces of Salih, the Arab trackers reading the details of all the camels he had brought with him from their tracks in the sand. "The sands are a public diary that even he who runs may read, for all living creatures go unshod," Thomas noted. "No bird may alight, no wild beast or insect pass, but needs must leave its history in the sands."

After Thomas finally linked up again with Salih, he faced the problem of paying off his Arab companions. The plan was that the group would now be guided by Hamad bin Hadi, a sheikh of the Murri tribe Salih had found. He would lead them through the sands of Dakaka to the water-hole of Shanna, where the third relay would begin. First, though, Thomas had to settle accounts with the Arabs who were leaving at Dhahiya. He had calculated an average of fifty Maria Theresa dollars for each man with his camel, and another forty for every pack animal, and spent several hours arranging the money meticulously into small piles. That, however, was not enough. First of all, the money had to be redistributed by Salih before anyone was satisfied — and even then, he faced demands for food from the Arabs who were leaving. But rations had been carefully calculated: there was another six weeks march ahead, and no more than six weeks' supplies in the saddle bags. Giving food away would mean that the expedition could not succeed — and so Thomas dipped once more into his bag of silver dollars, and each man got an extra two or three to see him on his way.

Compared with the privations they had suffered, and those that were still ahead, the trek that followed through Dakaka sounds occasionally like a desert paradise. There had been heavy rains, and so there was almost unlimited pasture for the camels — and for the men, there were golden hares under practically every bush. The Arabs would dig out their holes by hand, emerging triumphant with the struggling animals, which were then briskly dispatched and eaten.

All the time, though, Thomas was checking and rechecking his calculations. From Shanna, there were still three hundred and thirty miles to cover to reach Doha: the rations they had with them would barely be enough. There was no margin for error or mishap. "Perfect health in camel and man was essential; marches must be long and sharp; loss of camel, sickness, treachery, or tribal opposition or too slow progress might spell disaster," he noted stoically.

Dakaka had been composed mainly of sweeping red landscapes of hard sand, with dunes running in all directions, but after they left Suwahib, the colours became more muted, and the terrain softer — "a wide expanse of pale sands in the mood of an ocean calm" — with occasional scrub of hadh bushes. Here, the climate had been less kind: the Murri tribesmen could remember grazing their animals across this region, but now, after four waterless years, Thomas found nothing but "a hungry void, and an abode of death to whoever should loiter there". It was a grim reason for yet more checking of supplies and calculations.

The heading now was constantly north-west, towards the deep waterhole of Sanam — but reports of tribesmen in the region caused a lengthy detour. The concern now was not only with chance raiders, but with the possibility of word leaking out that a Christian traveller was in the area. Hostility might still be caused by the simple hope of plunder, but also now by the fear among the Arabs which Thomas records that he might prove to be the advance guard of a bigger and less well intentioned party of invaders. He had already described the unimaginable miseries of the English winter — the mystery, for instance, of ponds frozen over so that men could walk across them. What could be more natural than that people unfortunate enough to live in such a climate should seek to leave it and move in force into their own more welcoming land?

As Thomas struggled through the desert, that might have seemed an unlikely development — although, sixty-five years later, the popularity of the Gulf states among western expatriates suggests that it might not have been that far-fetched a possibility. For the moment, though, discomfort was added to toil and danger. In the sandhills of Ubaila, Thomas had his first experience of a desert sandstorm as he sat with his companions around their campfire.

"Suddenly the flames swept this way and that as though the wind blew from everywhere in turn. We all covered our faces with our hands to save our eyes from the smoke... The storm grew fiercer; the bedouin, with their poor mantles wrapped around them, huddled together for warmth... When my face was exposed, the gritty blast struck it with the sharpness of a knife..."

For Thomas, the sandstorm was bad enough: apart from the discomfort he suffered, he left the campfire to find that his scientific instruments were all but useless: his camera had sand in it, and his two aneroid barometers no longer tallied. But for the Arabs, with their thin clothes, the discomfort was intensified. It is one moment in Thomas's book when the sheer grinding poverty of the guides on whom he relied becomes clear. Like all the travellers, and with cause, he talks often of the nobility and the toughness of the Arab tribesmen: but it is important to remember that those qualities were bought at the price of intense hardship — and that the stamina the Arabs might show in haggling over an extra dollar was well matched by their total lack of material possessions.

As they pushed on northwards Thomas was continually impressed by the Arabs' unshakable loyalty to each other. When they arrived at the waterhole of Banaiyan after a solid ten-and-a-half hour ride, the first to dismount refused to touch either food or water until their colleagues, several miles behind them, had joined them. And yet their loyalty was to the enterprise as much as to each other. Thomas noted that Rashidi tribesmen, while happy to guide the party through the territory that they knew, would not divulge the location of secret water-holes to their Murri colleagues, and the Murri took the same attitude towards them. Among the shifting alliances of the desert tribes, no-one knew whether today's friend might be tomorrow's enemy.

Banaiyan marked the start of the last stage of their journey, with the eighteen-day dash across the main sands of the Rub Al Khali behind them, and the sea just eighty miles ahead — but crossing the Empty

Quarter was always more than simply struggling across the sands themselves. The beginning and the end of the journey, on each side of the great desert, had dangers and difficulties of their own. Thomas's guides warned him that the northern tribes might be even more hostile than those of the territory they had just crossed. Even though they were short of supplies, any suspicious tracks would once more mean a lengthy detour to avoid any possibility of ambush.

For the next few days, they progressed over hard, gravelly steppe country, alternating with white salt plains and hills of sand — searching, as ever, for decent pastures to keep their camels alive. The guide who had taken over from Hamad bin Hadi, an Arab from the northern Murri called Talib, seemed less sure of his ground than Hamad had done. Promises of firewood and pasture just over each hilltop repeatedly came to nothing — mistakes, Thomas noted, that might have cost them their lives in the height of the summer. "One bedu in ten is a good guide," he wrote, "and one in fifty a reliable informant."

By the beginning of February the journey was near its end. From the summit of a sand-hill, they could see the waters of the Gulf glistening in the distance. "The vast, almost uninhabited wastes of the Rub Al Khali stretched behind us, before us lay but a march of a few days to the dwellings of men," Thomas wrote. Slowly, the signs of civilisation multiplied: marks of camels in the sand, the distant sight of some of the animals grazing on a distant skyline, and then the footmarks of asses around the track on which they were travelling.

It was a miserable night, with no firewood and a steady, drizzling rain soaking the men and everything they had with them. That morning, Thomas took his breakfast cowering beneath his table in an effort to keep out of the chilling rain: but by now, they knew that they were only a few hours from the end of their journey.

"The bedouin moved forward at a sharp pace, chanting the water chants. Our thirsty camels pricked up their ears with eager knowingness. The last sandhill was left behind..."

And finally, they saw the towers of Doha silhouetted against the sea in front of them. While the bombastic adventurer, Philby, was still struggling to make his preparations, the quiet civil servant had won the race.

The journey was over: the Rub Al Khali had finally been crossed.

SERVANT OF THE KING

"To my companions and the great beasts that bore us —
hungering and thirsting but uncomplaining — the credit
of a great adventure"

          – H St J Philby

Philby's words at the end of his expedition sound more generous than anything that came before or during it. If his camels were uncomplaining, they were the only living creatures on the journey that were, and his free-handed renunciation of credit when the adventure was over contrasts ironically with his fractious bullying on the march.

Perhaps, with the hardships and triumph behind him, he could find more geniality in his soul. Certainly, his reaction before he set out to the news of Bertram Thomas's success seems to say more about his generosity of spirit: "Damn and blast Thomas!" he wrote.

On the one hand, the select group of travellers who had fallen under the spell of the desert shared a sense of fellow-feeling as like-minded colleagues, spreading the word of Arabia and Arabian life together to the rest of the world. Philby, like T E Lawrence, visited the ageing Wilfrid Blunt to pay homage to one of the pioneers of desert travel: he welcomed the discoveries of Thomas and the others like a true scientist, although he added pointedly that they had confirmed some of his own theories and reports.

The explorers' journeys were sometimes almost spiritual, virtually personal pilgrimages to the sands. Wilfred Thesiger, later, was to write lyrically of the unparalleled companionship he found among his bedu friends in the desert, while Philby himself describes his religious conversion in Arabia when, he says, "the great peace of Islam slowly and surely descended upon me, who had known no peace before..."

But there was, too, a search for personal glory. The Blunts were mortified when they discovered that Charles Doughty had beaten them to become the first undisguised European to visit Hail — and Philby knew well that the honour of the first recorded crossing of the Empty Quarter was the biggest prize of all, and that it had been snatched from his hands.

Later, after his first outburst, he was more restrained, but there was no hiding his disappointment that Thomas had pre-empted him. "He had won the race, and it only remained for me to finish the course," he wrote. He could, he says, have been the first to cross the sands himself, had it not been for the delays in obtaining permission from his master, ibn Saud. As Bertram Thomas was landing at Dhofar to make the preparations for his journey, ibn Saud and his advisers were agreeing that it would be wise to put off the expedition they had planned for Philby by a year.

At times, as he languished at court, he had begun to fear that he would never have his chance — but then, on January 7, 1932, he finally led his little caravan away from the oasis of Dulaiqiya — thirty-two camels and fifteen men, with another four guides to be picked up along the way. He had now no hope of winning fame as the first European to find a way across the Empty Quarter, but he was preparing to achieve a personal ambition which had obsessed him for fifteen years.

Philby, of course, was already a seasoned desert traveller, and yet even he was surprised when he woke on the first full day of the expedition. It was freezing cold: skins of water, frozen solid, were ranged around the campfire to thaw, and the thermometer carefully placed outside his tent showed five degrees of frost. "To think of such things in Arabia, proverbial for its fierce heat!... It was one of the coldest winters in the memory of living men," he wrote.

Until the journey was safely under way, Philby had been vague about his intentions, and when the rest of the party found that they were expected to make a pioneering journey across the Empty Quarter, they believed that their leader must be mad. They, after all, had none of Philby's hopes of recognition and glory from the scientific establishment in London, and their earnings from the entire trip, he admitted later, would amount to ten pounds or less each — enough to find themselves a wife, perhaps, but not to pay for a pedigree camel. "They groaned, some aloud and others silently, at the madness of it all. Homesickness accounted for much of their distress in those early days, but there was also a gripping fear at their hearts when mention was made of the Hadramaut and the Empty Quarter." The only reason to travel there, they said, was to hunt the oryx around the edge of the desert.

The first part of the journey, as far as the oasis of Jabrin, was planned as a way of breaking in the party — and particularly Philby himself — for the ordeal ahead. The camels themselves seemed to trek through the desert by instinct, falling automatically into single file as they made their way across soft sand, so that the following animals could tread, like Good King Wenceslas's page, safely in the tracks of the ones that went before; but, apart from one journey nine months before, it had been six years since Philby had been on a camel-saddle, and the unaccustomed exercise left him stiff and awkward.

They stayed a few days in Jabrin, exploring the abandoned hamlet with its mosque half-buried in the drifting sand, and picking up occasional pottery shards and broken bangles, which Philby carefully squirrelled away, along with his geological specimens and dead moths and insects. The Arabs who had lived there, the guides explained, had fled the threat of fever and sickness in Jabrin to live in the surrounding desert, returning only to pick the dates from the neglected palms.

The news in the region was bad: the drought was unbroken, and there would be little hope of killing game to eke out their supplies. But Philby felt himself at the start of his life's adventure. Just as the Blunts had realised that they could not go back once they had crossed the Nafud Desert, so he knew leaving the oasis at Jabrin to be a moment of decision. Now there was no turning back: the only way was forward into the Rub Al Khali — a prospect which Philby claims filled him with rejoicing, but which left his companions sobered and depressed.

The way was fairly easy to begin with, journeying southwards across wide sandy valleys, until they reached the ridge of Dharbun. From the summit, they had their first panoramic view of the land they were setting out to cross — "a flat, featureless study in brown, with the black splash of our baggage animals seemingly crawling over it in the distance ahead". There had been no rain for almost nine months, but even so, there were plenty of green shoots on the bushes for the camels to crop as they ambled by. For Philby the naturalist, there were a few small birds, several hares and jerboas, and the tracks of foxes, and hyena — and even the fragments of a complete ostrich shell found lying in the sand.

When the Blunts had ridden through the Nafud some fifty years before, they were told that ostriches were still occasionally seen in the desert: now, the news for Philby was that the bird was finally extinct in Arabia. Ali, one of his guides, claimed that his father used to shoot them in the sands forty years before, although the others said that only the oldest men of the deserts had ever seen the creatures alive.

Philby collected the fragments of many shells, including several dating back to prehistoric times. "Who shall say for certain that the great bird does not survive in the remotest recesses of the wilderness," he pondered, optimistically.

On his travels, he collected a huge variety of samples and curiosities — pieces of rock, shells, skins, butterflies and insects — so that his companions became quite used to watching him patiently stalking some tiny creature which was quite invisible to them, clutching his killing bottle in his eager fingers.

At times, he seems almost to have played the role of some ghastly

Angel of Death for the birds, reptiles, and mammals he encountered. Where Thesiger, later, was to take photographs, Philby was content with nothing less than corpses: there is a pathetic description of a dying monitor lizard, its back broken by a gentle tap from Philby's riding cane, snapping helplessly in the sand, and it is only his lack of prowess as a marksman that seems to have prevented him from butchering every small bird that flew into sight. In that context, perhaps, his lament for the ostrich sounds a little ironic.

Moreover, Philby's collector's zeal was not always matched by scientific skill: he confesses that several of his prize specimens were ruined through not being properly preserved and looked after. Thesiger's photographs survived as a record of a vanished world: many of Philby's specimens, ironically, ended as nothing more than foul-smelling messes of putrefaction — a grisly memorial to the triumph of enthusiasm over experience.

The expedition was also, for him, a return to desert travellers' food. The journey was taking place during Ramadan, and Philby and some of his companions had decided not to take advantage of the licence allowed to travellers to postpone the fast. But even his hunger at the end of a day without food was not enough initially to whet his appetite for the broth that his companions prepared from the hares they had caught. "Nothing of such delicacies is wasted, and only the unextruded food in the intestines is squeezed out before the remaining contents of the stomach are thrown into the pot with the meat," he recorded dutifully. The others wondered at his squeamishness; indeed, later in the journey he began to join in the desert stew. Hunger, as other travellers discovered before and after him, can make the most unlikely dishes seem welcome, if not exactly appetising.

The following morning, he noted one of the unexpected attractions of the desert, beyond the spectacular scenery and the companionship of his Arab guides: the crisp cool of the air, which he compared with a late autumn in England. "There is something in the uncontaminated atmosphere of the desert that makes one actively conscious of health," he wrote enthusiastically. "Perhaps it is this that accounts for the 'lure of the desert', which cannot be cured in him that has once tasted of it."

The wells on which Philby's party relied were ones well-known to the bedu, carefully maintained over the years with leather caps laid across them to prevent the sand from blowing into them and filling them up. They were often dug centuries before: at Maqainama, for instance, the water was more than one hundred and seventy feet below the surface, leading Philby to conclude that it had been dug as part of a programme of works of some ancient civilisation, possibly connected with the traditional trading route that ran past it.

Even maintaining the water-holes, though, meant constant attention by the bedu who used them. The mouths of the wells were often protected by a structure of woodwork and wattle which would occasionally need repair by a passing traveller. But the wellhead could easily get covered in sand, and the work then could be hard and dangerous. Digging down through the soft sand which might drift over it was only possible at all if the edge of the crater was kept constantly dampened to stop it sliding inwards — a precarious task at the best of times. The first few feet of the well might be lined with blocks of stone, as Philby found at Bir Fadhil, but the shaft sometimes went down below that for a hundred feet or more through sand, rock, and alluvial soil. A collapse would be virtually impossible for a lone traveller to clear, however desperately he might need the water at the bottom of the well: Philby's companions pointed out one ruined well at the foot of which they said lay the body of a man who had been buried by a fall of sand as he tried to dig down to the water.

Philby did not rely on word of mouth when it came to the water of Maqainama itself. It was reputed to be particularly sweet and good, and he made a detailed scientific study. The water was drawn to the surface in a bucket on the end of a long rope — items of equipment which were universal to the travelling bedu of the region — and the meticulous Philby decanted some into a bottle, which he sealed with wax and took home carefully for analysis. This after all, he had been told, was some of the purest water he would find in the desert. The analysis was less lyrical, if more precise. The water was highly polluted with camels' urine, with ammonia levels of something like six hundred times those found in water normally considered drinkable. "One can scarcely perhaps expect the west to appreciate the virtues of camel urine tempered by countless generations of seepage through sandstone rock," he observed wryly.

But whatever the quality of the water according to the analysts, the wells could and did save the lives of bedu and other desert travellers, although they could also be a source of danger. The wells of Shanna, for instance, to which Philby came later in his journey, were situated at the meeting point of the tracks through the southern desert, which made them a favourite haunt of raiders and bandits. They were, he wrote, "a fount of life in the southern sands and equally for that reason, a source of death and danger. None approaches Shanna but with circumspection; none remains there, on the well itself, longer than may be necessary to water the beasts and fill the skins." The ghazal from which the Blunts had so luckily escaped with their lives and their property intact had come when they had paused by a well: watering the camels was a task best undertaken with a wary eye kept open for strangers.

As they journeyed on towards the province of Aflaj, there was a graphic reminder of the dangers that might lurk in the dark of a desert night. Philby was summoned to dinner, he says — like many of the explorers, he seems to have expected the services of an entire household staff to attend to his comforts even in the middle of the desert — to find the whole party tense and armed to the teeth. "It was a wonderful scene under the full moon that night, nearly a score of hardened desert veterans gathered around our piled-up tray of rice and meat, half squatting, half-kneeling, rifles in hand and bandoliers at waist. With their free right hands, they ladled the food into their mouths, while their senses were taut…" One of them had smelled the smoke of a camp-fire on the still night air; the faintest trace, but enough to convince them that other travellers, perhaps dangerous ones, were about. It was, says Philby, the first time that he had realised that a highly-developed sense of smell was one of the hallmarks of the desert traveller. Later, they heard that there had indeed been a gang of brigands in the area: perhaps their warlike preparations had frightened them off.

From Maqainama on to Aflaj was some four days' journey along old camel-drivers' routes, first across the bare, broken uplands of Summan, and then into the sands of the Dahna Desert, the same desert which Palgrave had struggled across on his journey towards Hofuf seventy years before. Philby's next objective was the lost city of Wabar, or Ubar: if Thomas had beaten him in crossing the Empty Quarter, Philby may have reasoned, there was still the prize of the first discovery of the legendary desert city, destroyed by fire from heaven because of the licentiousness of its people.

For much of the way across the sand, Philby walked beside his camel, fretting over the pace, which he calculated at around three miles an hour, but also pausing at the wayside occasionally to stalk another moth or insect, killing-bottle in hand, or to pluck a new plant for his collection. He claimed later that, of twenty-four different species of moths he collected on his travels, sixteen were regarded by scientists in London as new to science.

As the procession advanced towards its goal, they crossed from the sand onto gravel plains, which forced the barefooted Philby back up onto the back of his camel. The camels themselves suffered in silence, although the sharp stones tore their delicate feet to ribbons. The treatment was effective but brutal: strong men would hold the struggling animal on the sand, while a 'cobbler' stitched a patch of butter-softened leather onto its foot. It sounds agonisingly cruel — and yet, claims Philby, the camel would get up from its ordeal apparently none the worse for it.

After the gravel came an area of soft, billowing dunes, which left the party strung out in a long line, struggling up and down the treacherous sandy slopes. The guide, Zayid, and two or three of the other Arabs rode far ahead, talking volubly; behind came another Arab, riding alone and reciting passages from the Qura'n as Ramadan devotions. Then came Philby and his servant, deep in conversation, with the rest far behind, chanting a travellers' song as they trudged along.

The most exciting find along the way, for Philby at least, was a litter of shells, with what appeared to be prehistoric flint tools scattered among them. It was, for anyone used to considering the study of antiquity in the crowded lands of the west, where the treasures and the rubbish of one generation are piled upon those of the ones before, an astonishing discovery. "The flint implements found in association with the shells set me off imagining ancient man in occupation of the banks of an old river or lake, or visiting them to hunt with spears and arrows the beasts that came down to drink," Philby wrote excitedly. Even more than that, it raised his hopes for the lost city to fever pitch.

Ali, one of the guides, had ridden on ahead: now he came hurrying back, waving excitedly. He had found the two castles, he said, and, although they were sometimes buried in the dunes, they were now standing further out of the sand than he had ever seen them. To prove it, he had brought with him a stone from one of them — a blue-black, squarish glassy block. Philby's first glimpse of the lost city was a "thin, low line of ruins riding upon a wave of the yellow sands", and, having taken a photograph, he hurried towards it in excitement. His triumph was short-lived. "I reached the summit, and in that moment fathomed the legend of Wabar. I looked down not upon the ruins of an ancient city, but into the mouth of a volcano, whose twin craters, half-filled with drifted sand, lay side by side, surrounded by slag and lava outpoured from the bowels of the earth."

For a man whose hopes of being first to cross the Empty Quarter had already been dashed, it was another bitter disappointment: it was to be nearly sixty years later, three decades after Philby's death, before fresh evidence of the legendary city and its fate appeared.

But there was no time to indulge his despondency. Philby had to make do with the discovery of a twenty-five-pound block of meteoric iron — a disappointment itself after the stories he had been told of a piece of iron the size of a camel — and prepare for the long, waterless journey to Ain Sala. With only an hour's break, the little party marched on from the early morning to the middle of the afternoon, through a bare, windswept landscape where the sand whipped their faces.

As they went south over the next few days, the waves of sand dunes gradually became grander to look at, and harder to climb, with soft, cloying sand sucking at the camels feet as they plodded along; but the valleys between them were correspondingly more fertile. They were traces of gazelle and oryx, as well as birds and insects for Philby's collection.

Now, though, came the first signs of open rebellion among the group. Four days out from Wabar, and with Ain Sala still a good forty miles away, the waterskins were practically empty — the result, an angry Philby claimed, of careless prodigality with what should have been an adequate supply for a six days' march. His plan was to head straight on for Ain Sala, water or no, but two of his party slipped away in the night to head for a well some distance away. In fact, they were held up by a sandstorm in the night, and had to rejoin the main group a few hours later, but it was the first sign of the wrangling that was to lead to Philby's next disappointment.

The following night, the look-out reported strange sounds in the darkness around their camp — raiders, perhaps, or even malevolent desert spirits. With the worst of the march still before them, enthusiasm was ebbing from the tiny caravan with the dwindling water-supply. But the next day, finishing the last of their water with their morning coffee, they had only fifteen miles to cover before they reached the oasis: a patch of bare rock in a two-hundred-foot depression in the sand. It was to prove yet another disappointment.

The well itself, a two-foot shaft some fifty feet deep, was sunk through solid sandstone rock, but it had fallen into disrepair and had been abandoned to the blowing sands. The only water to be found had to be carried in skins from the wells at Naifa, some miles away.

It was on an expedition from Ain Sala that Philby first experienced the phenomenon of the 'singing sands', which Thomas had heard before and which Thesiger was to hear after him. It was, he admitted, something that the bedu were quite used to, although there was no clear explanation of its cause.

The party was camped in a hollow between a group of sand-dunes, with one of the guides sitting on the crest of a ridge. "Quite suddenly, the great amphitheatre began to boom and drone with a sound not unlike that of a siren or perhaps an aeroplane engine — quite a musical, pleasing, rhythmic sound of astonishing depth," he wrote afterwards.

The 'performance', which Philby's guides explained as the working of the spirits of the desert, went on for about four minutes, and Philby more prosaically ascribed it to the noise of the sand, disturbed by the man on the ridge and sliding down the steep slope. As it began to slip downwards, there was a faint grating noise, but it was not until the shifting mass of sand had moved some fifty feet down the slope that the note suddenly changed and the musical boom began.

For Philby, the experience was small comfort for the disappointment that had started his journey, or the anti-climactic discovery of the 'ruined city' of Wabar; but his excitement at what he called the 'sand concert' shows him at his most attractive, hurrying around the campsite with his bottle to collect samples of the sand, while trying almost like a small boy to start the singing again and again. "I thrust the bottle deep into the soft, moving, singing sand and, as I drew it out, noticed a remarkable suctional sound as of a trombone... Furthermore, as I knelt on the moving sand, I experienced a curious but quite unmistakable sensation of a subsurface throbbing and pulsing, as in a mild earthquake." It is a brief glimpse of the passion which marks almost all the desert explorers — a small clue, perhaps, to why they made their journeys.

Philby's preference for walking rather than riding his camel was only partly in order to continue his search for insects and tiny plants: he also wanted to shame the others into pushing on a little faster. As they wandered on towards Ziqirt, the tension between him and his guides bubbled over briefly. "You are hot-tempered, and easily get angry if we do not as you please... and you are ever ready to disbelieve what the guides say," said one, in tones apparently more of sorrow than of anger.

Philby tried to explain his own anxiety to push ahead, and his distrust of guides who seemed to say whatever was most convenient at the time about their route or the time they should expect to take. "As for the heat in my heart," he said, "it may be that God put it there when he created me, but it is you folk that enflame it with your contrariness." It sounds to have been a fairly mild disagreement, but it was another sign that all was not well within the little group. There was, Philby noted quietly in his journal, a general desire to get home from the wilderness as quickly as possible, whether that meant abandoning the crossing or not.

At the wells of Shanna, they lingered nervously for two days, always aware of the danger of attack from raiders, even though they had taken the precaution of leaving a sketch of ibn Saud's mark in the sands to warn any potential enemies that they had the backing and protection of the king. At the wells, for the third time, fear and dissent burst to the surface. The group would not go further south into the desert: they would rather risk the anger of ibn Saud, terrible as that might be, than commit themselves to the waterless sands.

"We argued and wrangled. I protested that I would on no account go back to the Hasa. They could abandon me if they liked, but that would be very serious for them: they would get no reward from me, and would certainly have to face the direst wrath of those who had sent me," he wrote later. It says much for the honour of the bedu, and for Philby's own faith in the laws of the desert, that it seems to have occurred to no-one that they could have solved their problems by doing away with him and swearing to the king that he had died a natural death in the sands.

Instead, Philby reached a deal: if they would set out across the desert with him from there, he would not insist on travelling further south, which had been his original intention. It was a proposal, oiled with a judiciously offered bag of silver dollars, which seemed to win favour.

All of them declared they had never heard of any previous crossing from Shanna to the settlement of Sulaiyil, which is where they had decided to head for. Although hunters might range far and wide in the desert, returning to the wells occasionally for water, there was no point in setting out from one side to another. "It was and is perhaps difficult to believe that such a crossing had never been attempted or accomplished before just for fun or from sheer love of adventure," wrote Philby — perhaps encapsulating, unwittingly, one of the differences between himself and his companions. Certainly they showed no sign of seeing the enterprise as fun, or of being overwhelmed by the adventure of it. Desert travel, for them, was a hard and demanding way of life, rather than a way of winning fame.

The decision having been taken, preparations went on hurriedly. Thirty-two waterskins were patched and greased, and then filled from the well before being laid out overnight ready for inspection and loading the next day, while the camels themselves were given the chance to build up their strength in the relatively lush pastures of the valley. Though a light caravan would have been able to travel more easily than heavily laden camels, which would founder and struggle, they were unwilling to send back any of the camels with the heavy baggage — a decision, as Philby noted, which nearly led to disaster.

It was the morning of February 22 when they finally set off.

Nineteen men and a dog — they had been given a saluqi bitch earlier on the journey — along with thirty camels laden with food, water, and supplies, as well as boxes of Philby's precious specimens, were on their way into the sands. They had already travelled for nearly seven weeks across the desert, and, despite the pause at Shanna, both men and camels were exhausted and run down. "Little did they understand the joy that bubbled over in my heart as we breasted up to the great desert at last! As little did I fathom the dark scheming of their treacherous minds as they marched with me into the unknown," Philby wrote afterwards. There were more disappointments in store for him before he achieved his ambition.

Here and there on their route away from Shanna, they found small splashes of green andab grass, quickly disposed of by the hungry camels. The bedu explained to Philby that the andab grass was always the first to spring into life after a shower of rain, followed closely by the abal. The abal will survive the drought longest, they said; by observing the state of the various plants, they were able to say more or less accurately when the last rains had fallen. But as they made their way further into the desert, even the hardiest plants vanished from the landscape. They passed the horns of a doe oryx, lying on the ground where she had apparently died of hunger; a single eagle wheeled on the rising air-currents in the clear blue sky, searching vainly for some living thing to eat.

One of the Arab guides, looking out over the bare, desolate landscape, declared: "The Rub Al Khali they talked of to you, this is it! It is three years since any rain fell here, and you will find the zahr bushes no more until you come to Harmaliya, five or six days hence." As they plodded west, they were heading directly into the setting sun. It was, said Philby, like marching into a furnace.

It was after five days, with a third of the journey across the Empty Quarter behind them, that Philby faced mutiny among his colleagues. Four of the camels were close to collapse; the men would not continue with the forced daytime marches. Philby suggested that the party should split, with the baggage animals returning to Riyadh or Hofuf, while a light and well-equipped group made a final assault on the sands. In the end, though, faced with his colleagues' refusal to break the expedition up, he was compelled to agree to a general retreat to the wells at Naifa, some hundred and forty miles away. After resting, watering, and building up their strength there, he said, they could set out again.

For the present, though, the desert had defeated them. It was Philby's latest and cruellest disappointment, and, even though he admitted that they were faced with the very real possibility of a terrible death from thirst in the desert, he vented his spleen in a bitter attack on the rest of the party. "In such circumstances, the Arab does not show up to advantage. He clings frantically, desperately to life, however miserable, and when that is at risk, loses heart and head," he wrote savagely. The Arabs, had they seen what he was writing, might have added that it was their clinging to life which had enabled them to survive such harsh conditions at all — and that the reward and glory of what had seemed to them from the start to be a mad enterprise were all to be Philby's.

He saw himself, he says in an interesting sidelight on his own towering self-esteem, as a latter-day Moses, with the multitude clamouring against him. It was, he wrote, the worst day of the whole expedition — probably the most terrible of his life — and he comes out of it, by his own account, as a petulant and self-obsessed bully.

The journey back to Naifa was a considerable expedition in its own right, with water and supplies both running low as Philby and his companions followed their baggage animals back towards the east. For six days at a stretch, Philby ate nothing but dates, with an occasional sweet biscuit taken as a luxury with a cup of tea, until they came to a spot where one of the baggage camels had accidentally dropped a few onions, which were divided up and eaten with relish by the famished travellers.

The heavily-laden advance party in whose footsteps they were following were obviously struggling under their load, and four or five of the camels collapsed during the first day's marching. But Philby had now become utterly obsessed with his ambition of crossing the desert, even though it was now quite clear that the expedition might quite well end in failure and death for the entire party. "What of nineteen lives in comparison with the thousands sacrificed by every general that history has honoured?" he wrote afterwards — showing once again how distant he had become from his companions. By now, Philby was riding on his own, deliberately avoiding his companions. The owners of the other eighteen lives, had they been consulted, would certainly have had a different view of the matter.

The camels were only kept going at all by 'snuffing' them — forcing a little of the precious water up their noses in order, Philby says, to "cool their brains". The animals — "silly beasts", he called them — struggled against having water poured mercilessly into their nostrils, but it apparently proved quite efficacious. Even so, they fought to get into whatever shade was available whenever camp was pitched. "The camels looked unutterably miserable, and were indeed utterly exhausted, though happily unconscious of the supreme effort which they would shortly be called upon to make," said Philby, with an unusual degree of sympathy.

One of the females, in fact, was so affected by the march that she gave birth prematurely to a calf, an event awaited with excitement by the entire party. It was not sentiment that affected them: in fact, they had the fire lit and ready to cook the poor creature before it was even born.

For weeks, Philby had drunk nothing but weak tea and camel's milk: never in his life, he wrote, had he tasted nectar like the foul, briny water of Naifa which he drank when they finally struggled into the oasis, late at night. It was the first water to pass his lips for fifty-five days. Once again, the analyst's art in London put his ecstasy into context: the water proved to contain so much chloride that it would not have been considered drinkable in Europe. Even before that, Philby had his suspicions: inspection of the water skins when they had finished the crossing of the desert showed that the water had corroded the tough leather. Its effects on the digestive systems of the men who drank it can be imagined.

They spent several days at Naifa, resting and recovering. There were occasional welcome showers, and grazing for the camels, although one of them ended her sufferings in a rather more permanent way, and provided meat dinners for the whole party throughout their stay at the oasis and on the journey which followed it.

At last, Philby got his way: the party was to separate, with one group taking the baggage train across country to Riyadh, while he himself, with eight companions, went back to try the crossing to Sulaiyil again.

Perhaps it was the food, or perhaps it was the understandable satisfaction of having got his own way, but Philby ended the period of rest and recuperation in a better frame of mind than he had started it. He said goodbye to the Arabs leaving with the baggage train with real affection, and even admiration: "The farewell of the Arab is manly indeed. With fair words on his lips he strides off into the desert and is gone. He never looks back," he wrote. Some fifty years before, Charles Doughty had noted the same reserve, although he, characteristically, interpreted it differently. "The Arab, until now so gentle a companion, will turn his back with stony strange countenance, to leave thee for ever," wrote Doughty, adding that he found the habit "wonderfully ungracious". Philby, for all his self-regard and ill-humour, seems in this instance at least to have been more sympathetic to the Arab temper than his curmudgeonly predecessor.

It was evening when the nine companions set off to the north-west, the dunes shrouded in a damp mist, and an occasional gentle drizzle blowing into their faces. Ahead, they could see nothing but the silhouettes of the men in front, marching along in silence. This time, it seemed, all the omens were good: there was every hope of completing the crossing and travelling on to Mecca in time for the pilgrimage.

Like the explorers before him, Philby had good cause to reflect on the near-magical abilities of his guides. Often, he said, they did not know themselves how they found their way; perhaps, Philby suggested, they had some instinctive sense of direction, controlled by a subconscious awareness of the sun or the stars. At other times, though, what seemed to be either magic or instinct was simply the use of an encyclopaedic knowledge of the landmarks and the terrain of a particular region. "The desert man knows every dune and ridge and fold as the shepherd knows his individual sheep. From each one to the next he will guide you unerringly until you come to the desired objective, but from afar he may deceive you and himself if you ask him to point out its bearing," he wrote.

Elsewhere, the guide had apparently found his way through the treacherous sands at night by the feel of the sand on his feet, sensing whereabouts the soft and dangerous areas might be on the dune face. There were also signs to be read by observant trackers. In one incident, Ali, another of Philby's guides, picked up pieces of camel dung from the side of the track. It was in small hard pieces, he explained, the stuff of a camel that had been travelling a long way without water, not the rich, large droppings of camels wandering at pasture. It had also, he declared, been lying there for about a year, which meant it could well have been left by Bertram Thomas's expedition across the Empty Quarter, which would have passed along that route. Philby was convinced enough, or credulous enough, to add some of the pellets to his catholic collection of desert curios — a touching, if unconventional souvenir of the traveller who had beaten him.

In places, the drought had been unbroken for twenty years or more, but elsewhere there was enough grazing for the camels, and so for three days, they made their way easily along the track which had been so punishing before. "Then we were beaten and felt it; now, we were full of vigour and optimism, knowing that the real trouble lay ahead of us, but conscious that we had stolen a long march on it without much effect on ourselves," was Philby's analysis.

As they marched on through the early morning, he even had leisure to notice the soft light of the moon and stars, reflected off the dewy sand; bright enough to cast shadows, and to pick out each traveller in black silhouette against the skyline.

But by the time they had travelled some two hundred miles, or slightly more than half way across the desert, they were about as far from water in any direction as they could be anywhere in Arabia. There was, Philby noted with a grim satisfaction, no point in going in any direction other than forward. The camels were by now showing signs of thirst — "their ugly, pessimistic faces seeming to regard the desolate scene with disdain" — and had to be prevented from wandering off at every halt in an instinctive but hopeless search for water.

It was a desolate and awe-inspiring landscape, with occasional long tongues of sand licking out across the gravel in their path. "Death reigned supreme… A pile of whitened bones and a pair of horns, black and gracefully curved, betrayed the scene of a gazelle's last agony. We passed by the hole of a desert mouse, whose in-going tracks told us it was still at home, but we were too tired to dig it out," Philby wrote. With the camels in torment, and with no respite from the blazing sun, there was a very real possibility of a breakdown. It was the realisation that from such a halt, the party would never have got up, that their bones would have joined those of the gazelle, that kept them going; that, and the realisation that they still had plenty of water, as long as it was used sparingly. There would even be enough to 'snuff' the camels at the evening campsite.

By now, even Philby himself was feeling the strain: he was beginning to wonder whether he could manage another day on the waterless diet he had imposed on himself. After an argument a few days before, he had sworn not to touch milk for the rest of the journey: now he was surviving on a few dates and a little raw meat each day, with five small pots of tea — perhaps a total of four pints of water.

Half an hour after midnight, they were off again. The evening hours in the cool were too precious to waste in sleeping. As they moved on, the ground was gradually becoming more and more stony, and finally they looked out from a low sandy ridge over a wide dark gravel plain that spread before them like an ocean. It was, the guides told him, Abu Bahr, the Father of the Sea. At that stage, they had little idea of how far it stretched, or of the long and painful hours they were to spend struggling across it; but even so, there was some hesitation in their steps as they set off slowly across the wide, dead expanse.

Philby makes no mention now of rejoicing as they set out across the plain. Even the guide, Salim, was uneasy at the thought of the long miles without fuel: it was more than anything the lack of coffee that concerned him, as there was no prospect of finding any wood for camp fires anywhere in the stony waste.

The Arabs, experienced riders that they were, dozed as their camels plodded on across the unending gravel. Even Salim seemed asleep, occasionally starting awake to indicate the line they should be taking, although, with no visible landmark to steer by, there was nothing to show how he was finding his way.

Finally, Philby's resolve not to drink water cracked. He had been eating onions and sucking peppermints to keep the worst pangs of thirst at bay, but after ten hours without liquid, he succumbed to the offer of a drink from one of his companions' skins. The water was tepid and dark brown in colour, but he drained the bowl without regret. He had been beaten by the desert, and he saw little disgrace in that.

They marched on, through the day, always into the setting sun. "Never in all my experience have I seen men drive and camels march as they drove and marched that day while there remained light to bring them to camp and fodder and fuel before nightfall," Philby wrote. But even sunset brought no rest: a brief pause for the sunset prayer was all

Zayid would allow, and they continued with their forced march, walking and trotting in turns.

Philby was growing testy as he longed to camp for the night: the Arabs seemed to have nothing on their minds but the need for coffee, while he could think only of how tired he was. After all, he argued petulantly, they had been dozing on their camels; and their need of refreshment could be no greater than his. Eventually, he stopped his camel and declared that he was staying for the night whatever the rest decided. Zayid cursed but agreed, and after twenty-one hours of practically ceaseless marching, they rested for the night, the camels stretching their long necks gratefully into the sand.

Philby, meanwhile, called over one of his companions, telling him he had two tins of fruit in his saddlebag, saved for emergencies. The two of them, he suggested, could share it secretly, without telling the others — it would, after all, have satisfied no-one if shared among all eleven. It was a practical argument, but not one that reflects well on Philby: it is hard to imagine Thesiger, for instance, sneaking a quiet bite while his friends went hungry. But Philby had no qualms. "The fruit and juice were lukewarm with the day's heating, but delicious, and I lay down to sleep as I had never slept before, while the clouds gathered about us with the music of distant thunder." At last, it seemed, they had broken the back of the desert. There were a hundred miles or so still to travel, but the worst of the journey was surely behind them.

Certainly, as they came upon the first few green shoots of 'arrad, the camels thought so. It was the first edible vegetation they had seen for two days or more. "No power on earth could have got our camels past them. Their hunger was terrible to watch, and we gave them their heads to do as they willed until they had made an end of the scanty herbs," Philby wrote.

As they passed into the sands of Rumaila, there were more and more desert plants; abal, hadh, and green shoots of andab, which the grateful camels cropped as they went. For the men, there was at last fuel with which to make a fire, but there were still few enough supplies with which to celebrate. They made the most of a few dates, washed down with their first tea and coffee for more than twenty-four hours. That night, there was a dish of rice to supplement the meagre rations of dates and raw meat to which they had become accustomed; and for Philby and his favoured companion, there was a second clandestine titbit of tinned peaches. Once again they had no second thoughts at all as they secretly wolfed the sweet fruit in the darkness.

Again, they started their march by night, but this time, as they loaded their camels soon after one thirty in the morning, they knew it was for the final stage of their expedition. As the grey dawn light gradually broke, they looked out on a gravel plain striped with green bushes. The camels were still famished, but remarkably choosy in what they devoured: they ignored the poisonous harmal, and also the acacia bushes, but jostled each other anxiously in their efforts to get at the occasional patches of dried-up grass — only a few mouthfuls each, but apparently enough to assuage the worst pangs of hunger.

Salim admitted that he had never travelled so long without food for his camels. "Without fresh fodder, they become thirsty, and when they are very thirsty, they cannot eat until they drink... they could last five days, perhaps six, without food, but that would be their limit. After that, they would just sit down and die," he said in a matter-of-fact tone. He did not need to add that, if the camels lay down and died, the men who accompanied them would not be far behind them.

But, after his setbacks and frustrations, fate had a small triumph in store for Philby. To his unconcealed delight, Zayid started to take a wrong direction; and after a few miles, even Salim confessed that he could no longer be sure of the way. Ironically, at the end of a journey for which the entire party had relied on the traditional skills of the Arab guides, they were reduced to faith in Philby's compass.

There was one more night to spend in the desert; in the morning, the little group awoke to the sound of birds in the bushes and trees around them. It was, said Philby with a degree of understatement, a pleasant change from the silence they had known before. They said their prayers

— throughout the whole journey, none of the party had missed a single prayer-time — and sent messengers ahead to the astonished mayor of Sulaiyil, with orders for a substantial meal to be prepared for them. After two and a half months with only occasional pickings of meat, they yearned for a good fat lamb, and even more, for hot, fresh bread.

The messengers left, and the rest of the party hurried on behind them. "Birds sang and twittered in the branches, and swallows swooped low along the ground, snapping up the insects that hummed gently among the flowers of spring. It was indeed a charming scene. And at last we saw a building of the sons of men, a little round watchtower…"

As they came into Sulaiyil, there were tamarisk trees, wells with villagers straining at the ropes to haul up the bulging water-skins, and willing hands to prepare coffee and tea for the travellers, and trays of water for the long-suffering camels — which, too thirsty to drink much, lapped cautiously at the tepid liquid. They had travelled three hundred and seventy-five miles from their last water supply. The expedition across the desert was over.

BROTHERS IN THE SANDS

*"I did not go to the Arabian desert to collect plants, nor to
make a map… I went there to find peace in the hardship of
desert travel and the company of desert peoples."*

– Wilfred Thesiger, *Arabian Sands*

In 1990, just twelve years after he had left Arabia for what he must have
believed was the last time, flying away from a new world of helicopters,
oil-fields, dual carriageways and fast-food restaurants, Wilfred Thesiger
came back to the Gulf. He had left in some bitterness: Abu Dhabi, the
simple coastal settlement towards which he had struggled across the
Empty Quarter more than thirty years previously, had grown almost
beyond recognition into the gleaming, modern capital city it now is.
"An Arabian nightmare, the final disillusionment," he called it. And yet
he came back.

His welcome was cordial, if a little bemused: like a favourite but
elderly uncle at a disco, the gentle, craggy-faced explorer seemed to
belong to a different world from the busy commercial metropolis his
hosts now inhabited; a world that was remembered nostalgically and
with pride, but one which definitely belonged to the past.

It was almost with an effort of will that he made his peace with the
country which he had loved, and then rejected. "I can personally regret
what's happened, and feel I was happiest in the desert with the bedu,
but in a changing world, they have to get the benefits they can. There
are hospitals here now, and schools," he said. "But I sense that they
have lost the freedom that they had — the freedom of the desert. The
bedu were always above everyone else: they were more civilised and

more noble, and they despised the villagers, the cultivators, and the townsmen. The highest standards of behaviour were the standards of the desert."

Outside was the noise of traffic on the main road: the tall, angular figure shifted uneasily in his armchair. He seemed as uncomfortable in it as he once admitted to feeling in the twentieth century — "old stone age man", he once called himself.

"Everything that is good about the Arabs has come to them from the desert," he said. "The only society in which I've found nobility is that of the bedu."

It all began, in a way, with the locusts. The fat, ungainly insects which so astonished his predecessors in the desert when treated as a tasty delicacy by the Arabs provided Thesiger with what he called his "golden key to Arabia". The Food and Agriculture Organisation wanted someone to collect information on whether the locusts bred in South Arabia, and if so, where, so that they could take more effective action to help the Arab farmers: Thesiger, who had already travelled in Abyssinia and the Sahara, only had to be asked once. "All my past had been but a prelude for the five years that lay before me," he wrote.

The journey to investigate the locusts took him to the Sands of Ghanim, on the northern slopes of the Jebel Akhdar; but, more importantly, it provided his introduction to the Bait Kathir and the Rashid, the tribes which were to provide most of his companions on his two journeys across the desert, and in particular, to Salim Bin Kabina, his inseparable companion in his Arabian travels over the next five years.

It also gave him a chance to practise his desert travelling skills. Like Philby, he found a seven-year gap in his experience of riding camels now left him stiff and sore at the end of a day's journey. But his commitment to travel at walking pace was already complete: "I had no desire to travel faster... there was time to notice things — a grasshopper under a bush, a dead swallow on the ground, the tracks of a hare, a bird's nest, the shape and colour of ripples on the sand, the bloom of tiny seedlings pushing through the soil," he wrote. The delicate mastery of detail which is a feature of *Arabian Sands*, his masterpiece of travel writing, was already planted firmly in Thesiger's character.

It was the following year before he returned to Salalah, on the southern coast of Oman, after months travelling around the Hejaz mountains. Once again, the experts at the Locust Research Centre had commissioned him to investigate possible breeding grounds for the insects in Oman — but this time, Thesiger was determined not to miss the chance to strike out across the Empty Quarter on a journey of his own.

He was not, of course, travelling in disguise — or at least, not yet. But he was anxious that the Sultan's authorities in Oman might get wind of his plan and forbid it, and so he did keep his ultimate destination a secret, even from the Bait Kathir tribesmen who set out with him.

Shortly after Shis'r well, the little group met up with the Rashid tribesmen who Thesiger hoped would escort him across the desert, and he had to admit to his plans. The Bait Kathir tribesmen were adamant: it would be a disgrace to allow him to travel on without at least some of them accompanying him as an escort, and so it was settled. A party of fourteen set off for the Empty Quarter: Thesiger, seven Bait Kathir, and six Rashid.

Far away, on the other side of the Arabian peninsula, were the oases of Liwa. They had never been visited by a European before, and even to the bedu accompanying Thesiger, they seemed almost to mark the limits of the known world; but it was to Liwa that Thesiger had decided to head. Before the party reached there, however, it would have to cross the Uruq al Shaiba, rolling sand mountains which blocked their way north. It was four hundred miles of hard, treacherous terrain, in the blazing sun — maybe a month before they could rely on finding any fresh supplies.

The calculations as the party set out were less than encouraging: they were short of food, so they could plan on no more than half a pound of flour each a day, and the camels could carry no more than twenty days' supplies of water. "If we did not find grazing, the camels would collapse, and that would be the end of us all," Thesiger wrote calmly. "It is the possible collapse of their camels which haunts the bedu. If this happens, death is certain. I asked al Auf what he thought: would we find grazing? 'God knows,' he answered."

The first few days took them towards Ghanim, over terrain already familiar to Thesiger from his previous year's travels. Occasional isolated dunes reared up in their path, apparently at random, but all with their steep faces pointing inexorably towards the north. His photographer's eye was avid for the tiniest details of shape, movement, or colour: "The surface of the sand was marked with diminutive ripples, of which the ridges were built from the heavier and darker grains, while the hollows were filled with the smaller, paler-coloured stuff... It is this blending of two colours which gives such depth and richness to the Sands: gold with silver, orange with cream, brick-red with white, burnt-brown with pink, yellow with grey. They have an infinite variety of shades and colours..."

By now he was absorbed in his Arab companions — in their friendliness, in their generosity. He never, he said, felt lonely in the desert, or anywhere among Arabs, and his one bleak hope was that Arab visitors to England would realise that westerners were as unfriendly to each other as they must appear to others. But there were other, less welcome, companions, apart from the tribesmen in his party: large, green scorpions, snakes which lay hidden in shallow burrows in the sand, and — entirely harmless but worst of all for Thesiger — three-inch spiders, with hairy, reddish legs, scuttling about in the firelight.

The Empty Quarter itself still lay ahead of them. As they camped one night on the edge of the rolling sand-sea, the Bait Kathir tribesmen sat apart for a while. The camels would not complete the journey, they said, and the danger of raiders on the other side of the desert was too great. The party would have to turn back, and settle for hunting oryx on the coastal plain. Only four of the tribesmen agreed to go on: two Rashid and two Bait Kathir would accompany Thesiger into the desert. They could take enough water to allow themselves a pint a day, and a spare camel which could be killed to provide meat if necessary. "I felt more confident than I had felt for days," Thesiger wrote that night, as he drank a bowl of soothing camel's milk. Unlike Thomas or Philby before him, he was able to press ahead with his journey.

The first dunes were brick-red, rising above ash-coloured plains of gypsum, with bright green salt-bushes, but as they plodded on, the colour softened to a gentle shade of honey, the dunes grew taller and steeper, and the vegetation gradually disappeared. It was sunset before they stopped to drink: water mixed with camel's milk for the Arabs, and boiled into tea with cinnamon, cardamom, ginger and cloves for Thesiger. For food, they shared about three pounds of flour scooped out of a goatskin and kneaded into gritty loaves of bread to be dipped in a little melted butter. That, with a few cups of coffee and a lot of late-night conversation, was their ration for the day.

Throughout the next day, they watched in anguish as their precious water dripped slowly through a leak in one of the skins, a drop falling onto the sands every few yards. And Thesiger was suffering: at the end of the day he was weak from hunger, almost crippled by stiffness after hours spent on his camel's back, and always conscious of his thirst, and of the slowly dripping goatskin. Even worse, though, was the knowledge of what lay ahead. It was not the distance they had to travel, but the great sand dunes of the Uruq al Shaiba that might defeat them.

After a few hours' sleep, they were off again in the early morning, feet stinging from the jagged salt-crusts on the ground. A few hours later they would be faced by a seemingly impenetrable chain of sand-dunes, and their guide, Mohammed Al Auf of the Rashid, set off ahead to try and find a way through. There was no way around, and no water to spare on lengthening the journey even if there had: all they could do was climb, man and camel united in a bizarre and energy-sapping pas de deux. "Very slowly, a foot at a time, we coaxed the unwilling beast upward. Each time we stopped, I looked up at the crests where the rising wind was blowing streamers of sand into the void, and wondered how we should ever reach the top."

And then, suddenly, they were at the summit, looking out over a rolling landscape of sand with shallow valleys and low hills. Thesiger sighed with relief: they had, it seemed, fought their way past the Uruq al Shaiba. It was several hours before anyone disabused him. "Did you think what we crossed today was the Uruq al Shaiba? That was only a dune. You will see them tomorrow," said Al Auf, as they paused to rest the camels. It was midnight before they stopped that night, and the worst, which Thesiger thought they had conquered, still lay ahead.

When they rose, the morning star was hanging above the dark shadows of the dunes, and the sand beneath their feet was like frozen snow. The dunes they faced now were higher than the previous day's, and the camels were trembling with exhaustion.

Earlier in his journeying, he had been convinced of the efficiency of the bedu's own travelling gear — the small, swinging lizard-skins of butter, for instance, or the goat-skins, also smeared with butter, in which water was carried, and which were mended when they leaked with tiny thorn plugs, wrapped around with a few threads of cloth. Now, as the camels were manhandled up the steep slopes, Thesiger and his companions had to carry the various bundles of food and provisions on their own shoulders. "As I struggled up the slope, knee-deep in shifting sand, my heart thumped wildly and my thirst grew worse. I found it difficult to swallow: even my ears felt blocked, and yet I knew it would be many intolerable hours before I could drink," he wrote.

They reached the top after three hours to find not the rolling landscape of yesterday, but instead, three more chains of sand dunes, with the ground falling away beyond them into a deep trough at the foot of a mountain of sand even higher than the one they had just crossed. It was one of Thesiger's few moments of despair. There was, he thought, no possibility of getting the camels over the far dunes, and no chance either of turning back the way they had come. There seemed nothing in store but defeat and death.

Once again, though, it was the quiet, unassuming confidence of his companions that proved right: "Somehow — I will never know how the camels did it — we got up the other side. There, utterly exhausted, we collapsed."

Al Auf doled out a little water as a reward — just enough to wet the travellers' dry, cracking lips — and they rested for a couple of hours, knowing that this time, the worst really was behind them. In front, there were still chains of sand dunes, but for the next few hours, until long after midnight, they threaded a way between them, following the valleys and avoiding the towering slopes above.

But now there was another danger. As they moved further north, they were coming to an area where tribal raids were at their height, and the local Arabs would be on their guard. Thesiger knew that, as an unauthorised foreign visitor and a Christian, he must keep news of his presence from spreading among the tribesmen and reaching the local governor. They would have to avoid all contact with other Arabs as much as possible, even setting up their camp when they arrived at Liwa out in the desert a little way from the oases.

The next day — fourteen days since they had left the Sands of Ghanim — two of the party went off to fetch water from a nearby well. It was slightly brackish, but delicious after the dregs they had been draining from the skins, and it meant they could drink extra cups of coffee after their meagre dinner of baked loaves. That was their celebration. The first part of their journey was over, and they had completed the crossing of the Empty Quarter — not, Thesiger admits, a journey of any great scientific or geographical importance, but a supreme personal achievement. Now, they only had to get back.

Their first problem was supplies. They were all close to starvation after their journey, and the only food they were able to get in Liwa was a few dates and a little wheat. The need to keep Thesiger's presence secret prevented the rest of the party from taking advantage of the hospitality that would have been available from the scattered bedu encampments.

To go near the town of Ibri, the next place where they might be able to buy food, would be to risk discovery, but it was unavoidable. For the Arabs, the enforced isolation was particularly hard, not so much because of the lack of food and hospitality as because it meant they would not be able to keep up with 'the news'. "Given a chance, the bedu will gossip for hours... and nothing is too trivial for them to recount. There is no reticence in the desert. If a man distinguishes himself, he knows that his fame will be widespread; if he disgraces himself he knows that the story of his shame will inevitably be heard in every encampment." It was being cut off from this exchange of stories and rumours that was hardest for them to bear — and it was in search of news that they were occasionally tempted to take the risk of approaching a stranger's encampment.

As they made their way steadily back towards Oman, the indistinguishable days stretched out monotonously from dawn to sunset. With the gravel plain stretching away always to the same vague horizon, distances became confused: often, dots which appeared to be far-off camels slowly making their way forward would resolve themselves after a while into a little group of stones in the track immediately ahead. There were no landmarks and, with the sun almost straight overhead, it was hard to see how the little party could find its way; and yet, after six long days, they finally rode up to the well at Haushi near the southern coast.

There, one of the camels which had been limping and suffering over the last few days provided them with a meagre supply of meat and even less fat. The Arabs loved their camels. "What other creature is as patient as a camel? That is the quality which above all else endears them to us Arabs," Bin Kabina observed to Thesiger during their later travelling. But that never blinded them to their severely practical use.

On this occasion, the only use of the weary camel was dinner — and barely enough dinner at that. But it saw them over the dead, empty miles to Bai, where they had arranged to meet the tribesmen who had turned back at the start of the journey. It was more than two months since they had seen each other, and they greeted one another as old friends and brothers, drinking coffee late into the night, and, even more important, exchanging 'the news'.

Thesiger's first crossing of the Empty Quarter was complete, and they made their way slowly back down the coast to Salalah.

The second journey, a year or so later, took him across the western sands of the Empty Quarter, in the opposite direction to the one St John Philby had chosen fifteen years before. Bin Kabina travelled to join him, as did Salim Bin Ghabaisha, a young Rashid tribesman who had joined them toward the end of Thesiger's earlier journey.

From the start, this was a more sombre expedition. The first leg would take them north from Manwakh to Sulaiyil, and all the warnings were that the Yam tribesmen of that region would kill the entire party — while the officers of ibn Saud, who maintained a post nearby, would be unlikely to welcome this unauthorised excursion into their domains.

The omens in other ways too were not encouraging: Thesiger slept uneasily, racked by nightmares of possible disasters, and even the camels had seemed unwilling to drink at the well ready for the sixteen-day journey to the next oasis.

The journey was long and gruelling, first across hard, flat sands, and then into gentle rolling sand-dunes, which sapped the strength of both camels and men. One camel collapsed, another was going lame in a shoulder, and all the rest were showing signs of exhaustion. It was only their good fortune in happening on an area of qassis to feed the camels that saved the entire expedition. With good grazing, they could slake their thirst just as well as with water. Had the plants not been there, several of them might well have died in the sands.

There were also plenty of oryx about, although even with the modern rifles Thesiger had provided, none of them managed to shoot one. They, he thought sadly, were almost certain to follow the ostrich into extinction once cars began to reach the hard sands and gravel plains where they live. The occasional shot from a group of travelling bedu hoping for a meal might not endanger their survival, but hunting parties shooting from fast-moving vehicles, and taking home piles of meat for sale, would wipe out the animal in a few years.

It was eleven days before they reached the most difficult part of the journey, the mountainous dunes of the Bani Maradh; soft red sand piled three to four hundred feet above them, and stretching away into the distance. This time, at least, it was the gentler slopes rather than the steep scarp slopes they had to climb, but even so, the camels had to be dragged and pushed upwards, and then held back as they plunged towards the bottom on the downward side.

There was the constant feeling that it was not just the terrain that was hostile: all the time, one of the party lingered behind, to check whether they were being followed by unfriendly tribesmen. But around them was nothing but silence, and they struggled forward for another three days over a flat gravel plain towards the Hassi well.

There, two of the party slipped away — as Saar tribesmen, they were in a special danger, as their tribe was at war with the locals — leaving Thesiger and his four Rashid companions to face the anger of ibn Saud. The guardian of the well was open about his dislike for Thesiger as a Christian, and for the Rashid as Muslims who had thrown in their lot with him, and he marched them straight off to the Emir at Sulaiyil. He seemed pleasant enough, although the jeers and the spitting on the ground of the local people recalled Doughty's unfriendly reception nearly seventy years before. Attitudes had changed very little in seven decades.

The Emir spelled out for them clearly how lucky they had been to survive. Ibn Saud had given permission for the tribesmen to take their revenge for recent raids on the Arabs of the south: any of them who had met the little group in the desert would have killed them out of hand. However, it seemed that their luck had run out. The word came back from ibn Saud that the entire party was to be imprisoned, and children in the street jeered that now the king would cut off the heads of the Christian and his companions. "I realised how badly I had misjudged our chances… I was so distressed that I could hardly speak. They had trusted me, and I wondered unhappily whether they were now going to suffer for it…"

It was Thesiger's fellow traveller Philby who saved them by interceding with ibn Saud on their behalf. They were to be released and sent on their way, and set off on the eight-day journey to the small town of Laila, over a track which had already been surveyed and mapped out by Philby — and, soon after their arrival there, the veteran Arabist himself walked into the house where they were staying.

He had arrived by car the day before, and set off to look for them in the desert; in fact, they discovered later, Thesiger had heard his car stuck in the sands, and even admitted to a certain grim satisfaction at the sound of the racing engine. Throughout his life, Thesiger had reserved his most vehement criticism for motor vehicles (although he might have moderated his dislike for this one occasion!)

Philby was an old friend, and the two desert explorers talked through the night. After he had left, Thesiger and his party spent another day preparing for the gruelling journey on to Jabrin and Abu Dhabi, a journey which, the local people informed them with glee, would certainly end in their deaths in the desert. This time, though, it was Thesiger's turn to impress his Arab companions. They were doubtful about their ability to find the way without local guides, but he assured them that he could manage with his compass and with the map that Philby had prepared.

Jabrin was eight days' riding away; after that, there were still four hundred miles to cover before they would reach Abu Dhabi. Thesiger's declared faith in his compass-reading was partly to instil confidence in the others. He had no knowledge of how reliable the maps he had were, and he knew only too well that he would only have to be ten miles out after their hundred and fifty mile trek to miss Jabrin altogether. They had few supplies, certainly not enough to provide for any extra travelling: if Thesiger's compass-reading failed to lead them to Jabrin, they would die.

After six days, they left the gravel plain and set out across the Dahna sands, and on the morning of the eighth day, they climbed a ridge, to find Jabrin spread out below them, just where Thesiger's calculations had predicted it should be.

But the hardest four hundred miles still lay ahead. They fed and watered the camels, filled their waterskins, and then set out again into the desert. Almost unbelievably, their problems now were the cold and the wet: their fingers were numbed with cold in the mornings, and there was a violent rainstorm overnight, and intermittent showers over the next few days. The Arabs called the rain 'God's bounty', and declared that it would yield rich grazing in the area for years to come.

Again, Thesiger's map and compass didn't let them down, and, even though the water at the single well marked on his map was too brackish for them to drink, it was good enough for the camels, and a day later they came upon a patch of grazing which, they declared, probably saved the lives not just of the camels, but of the whole party.

They spent five uncomfortable hours floundering through the salt flats of the Sabkha Mutti — dead, sterile, and treacherous terrain which left the camels struggling in thick black mud under the glaring salty crust — and then camped to make their plans. There was not enough water to head straight for Abu Dhabi, and no real prospect of meeting up with bedu who might know the whereabouts of more wells. All that could be done, declared Thesiger, was to strike out for Liwa.

The oases were about a hundred miles away, marked out in large letters across the map, but no European had ever been there. There was no reliable position for them, and if they missed the wells, they would be heading back out into the Empty Quarter, on a journey which could have only one end. It was a slim chance, but it was the only one they had.

This time, their success was due to a combination of Thesiger's compass and Bin Kabina's experience. Thesiger led them successfully in the right direction, but it was Bin Kabina who finally climbed to the summit of a dune and recognised the sands of Liwa in the distance. They were safe. In the settlements there, they found a guide who would take them on to Abu Dhabi. After the struggle against the threat of disaster, this final leg of the journey seems to have been something of an anti-climax — "a plodding weariness, during which we were inclined to quarrel over trifles".

But after making their way wearily along by the sea, over a drab, colourless coastal landscape, they struggled onto Abu Dhabi island on March 14. It was sixty-seven days since they had left Manwakh.

Search for the Lost City

"Some say the finest city in all Arabia was Ubar, built like
Paradise with pillars fashioned from gold…"

– Nashran bin Sultan

Thesiger's journeys continued for several months after his arrival in
Abu Dhabi, but he could sense the Arabia he knew slipping irresistibly
away. The modern world of motor transport, official documentation,
petrol and prosperity was changing the deserts almost before his eyes,
and in 1950, he writes, he boarded the plane for Europe, feeling as if he
were going into exile.

It requires only the slightest effort of imagination to understand how
he felt. He was a man who had been fortunate enough to find a world
in which he could be satisfied — but unlucky enough to see that world
begin to vanish like a mirage. In the four decades since he looked sadly
down from his aircraft on the changing coastline around Sharjah, the
door which he sensed to be closing has, in many ways, slammed shut.

Modern explorers claim to have uncovered the lost city of Wabar
which Thomas, Philby and the rest heard rumours of, and dreamed of
finding, but their triumph came at least partly because of the space
shuttle, satellite navigational technology, the reliability of the modern
four-wheel-drive and the black arts of PR and media relations, rather
than thanks to the courage and endurance of any epic desert journey.

Reflected light picked up in space gave archaeologists clues to
ancient trading routes that desert explorers could never have guessed
at — impertinent prying eyes from space spying on the desert stillness

— and in 1991, the explorer Ranulph Fiennes began in earnest the search on the ground for the lost city.

Fiennes's obsession with Ubar — even its name, whether Ubar or Wabar, was the subject of bitter disagreement among Arabists and explorers — began when he was serving in Oman as a soldier of the Sultan in the late Sixties. His patrols of the Dhofar region would occasionally wander inexplicably off towards the north and west around the Wadi Mitan, where he believed the lost city might be found; a cavalier attitude towards his military duties which he later admitted might, in harsher times, have ended with the explorer in front of a firing squad, accused of desertion.

But his first efforts to locate Ubar were amateurish, hit-and-miss affairs, without proper guides or preparation: a few soldiers asking tribesmen whom they chanced upon whether they had heard of the lost city; a few Landrovers bumping perilously over camel trails, or sinking into the treacherous soft sand and sabkha, hardly comprised an expedition in the tradition of Thomas or Thesiger. And there was all the time, at the back of Fiennes's mind, the thought that a serious breakdown would mean calling for official help and admitting to being miles from anywhere that he could reasonably plead fell within the area of his patrols.

His faith in serendipity is almost touching — the belief that a casual meeting with a guide was likely to lead him to the city that had eluded Thomas, Philby, and Thesiger before him. "With six Landrovers and a thousand miles of desert to our northern flank, I was superbly positioned to search for Ubar," he wrote later. It appears not to have crossed his mind that a thousand miles of desert could hide a hundred cities, and that six Landrovers could search for them at random for eternity without a hope of success.

And yet Fiennes seems never to have lost faith in the existence of Ubar; indeed, he took every opportunity to flesh out the hand-me-down stories of the local Arabs with some serious reading about the city, its legends and its history. Bertram Thomas, certainly, had heard about the city in great detail from the Arabs who accompanied him on his journey across the Empty Quarter. One of them told him, "It was a great city, our fathers have told us, that existed of old — a city rich in treasures, with date gardens, and a fort of red silver. It now lies buried in the sands… some few days to the north."

In the days when southern Arabia provided the rest of the world with frankincense, there were undoubtedly a number of towns in the Dhofar region which, allowing for the exaggeration of centuries of story-telling, could have fitted that description. They were trading centres, control points for the valuable spice caravans that passed through the territory on their way north, resting places for the weary camels, and the homes of wealthy and powerful kings and great families.

Merchants and travellers took home stories of immense opulence with them, and the geographers and scholars of ancient Alexandria mapped out a world which they can only have heard about in the vaguest terms. Claudius Ptolemy, for instance, preparing in the second century AD maps which formed the basis for the accepted geography of the world for hundreds of years to come, named one of the cities as Omanum Emporion, the market place of Oman — and positioned it confidently in the south-east of the Rub Al Khali.

The Qura'n, too, written down some five hundred years later, tells of desert cities — but of cities destroyed by God in punishment for their inhabitants' pride and sinfulness. The city of Irem, for example, was built according to legend in imitation of Paradise itself; retribution was terrible. "Consider how the Lord dealt with Ad, the people of Irem, adorned with lofty buildings the like of which has not been seen," says the Holy Qura'n. "All these cities, too big with pride, we did destroy. Against some we sent a sandstorm, some were seized by a great noise. For some we cleaved open the earth, and some were drowned."

But the memory of the ancient cities lived on. In the eleventh century, the Arab historian Al Himyari was still writing of great buildings smothered in sand in the deserts of southern Arabia. "Wabar is the name of the land which belonged to Ad," he wrote, apparently identifying not a single city, but an entire region.

The story of Ubar — of all the legendary cities of the southern Arabian desert, in fact — seems to be one of immense wealth suddenly and disastrously brought low. Certainly, climatic change would have played a part in that; Arab historians from the eighth to the thirteenth centuries all referred to Wabar as a fertile land with running water and luxuriant gardens. But the slow march of the desert is unlikely to have caused the sudden catastrophe of which the legends speak. Around the year 300 AD, the frankincense trade collapsed, precipitating an economic catastrophe for the cities which had built their wealth upon it. And on top of that, as Fiennes was to find later, was the likelihood of some natural disaster that could literally have shaken Ubar to its foundations.

One possibility that occurred to him was that the name of the city could have changed over the centuries, that Ptolemy's Omanum Emporion, the Irem of the Holy Qura'n, and the Ubar of popular legend could be one and the same place. All were reported to have been in the same area, serving the same caravan routes. That there should have been one single major city among the settlements of the region was at least a possibility.

But that speculation had little to do with Fiennes's day to day work. For all his reading and study — and despite his occasionally imaginative interpretation of orders about exactly where his platoon should be patrolling — his years in Oman were busy. During the unsettled years of the late 1960s, he was involved in ambushes and counter-insurgency work throughout the Dhofar region and, even though he managed to find time to lead an expedition up the White Nile, his ambition to find Ubar had to be shelved.

Occasionally, he would ask Omanis with whom he was working about the city. One of his guides, Nashran bin Sultan of the Bait Shaasa, had described it to him as "the finest city in all Arabia... built like

Paradise with pillars fashioned from gold" — and had even promised, not quite convincingly, to lead him to it.

Others were less encouraging. Said bin Ghia, another of the Sultan's intelligence agents, roared with laughter and described the stories of Ubar as nothing but rubbish. One bedu said there was a curse on the man who found it, and refused to have any part of the project; another led Fiennes on a three-day expedition into the sands, only to declare that the stone pillar he had promised to find had unaccountably disappeared. Still others talked knowledgeably, but refused all inducements to lead an expedition to the city. It was clear that if Ubar existed, there was nobody alive who had ever seen it.

One particular assignment sent Fiennes and his patrol into the gravelled plains, or Nej'd, that fringe the Empty Quarter, and appeared to offer another fortuitous opportunity to look for the lost city. Searching for water holes and safe military routes through the mountains would, he thought, leave time for a little unofficial prospecting on his own account. One idea he was anxious to test was that references by Bertram Thomas to a mysterious ancient track that seemed to vanish into the sands of the Empty Quarter could provide a crucial clue to the lost city. Thomas's own Arab guide had described one set of tracks as "the road to Ubar", and other bedu said that many tracks converged on the ancient city.

Corroboration seemed to come from a different and unrelated source: twenty-five years after Thomas, the American archaeologist Wendell Phillips also claimed to have seen the road to Ubar. "A well-marked highway centuries old, made by thousands of camel caravans, leads west for many miles from the famous spice lands of Dhofar and then, on a bearing of N75°W, mysteriously disappears without trace in the great sands," he said.

Fiennes suggested that the roads spotted by the two explorers were very likely the same, and in any case, it seemed probable that a city as grand as Ubar would have been at the centre of a network of routes. If it were possible to find those routes, he reasoned, it should be possible to find the city itself — the more so as he was working with a better-equipped team and more reliable vehicles.

Before they struck out into the sands, though, they paused briefly at the watering hole of Shis'r on the Wadi Ghadun, where a big limestone outcrop towered over the surrounding countryside, sheltering a spring far below it. On top of the outcrop was a modern Omani fort to guard the spring; close by was the crumbling ruin of an earlier building. Some of the Arabs said that the ruin might date back to the nineteenth century; other rumours, reported by Wendell Phillips, claimed it had been built three hundred years earlier, by a local sheikh, Bed'r bin Tuwairiq. Either way, it was of little interest to the explorers, and they paused only briefly before setting off on their quest. It was a pause Fiennes was to remember years later.

Once in the sands and away from the gravels of the Nej'd, there was little life to be seen. Occasionally lizards and insects crossed their path, but there were neither mammals nor birds; certainly none of the deer or partridge with which they had eked out their rations before.

In the Nej'd, Fiennes — like the Blunts, Doughty and all the other travellers of Arabia — found the local wildlife fascinating and not always welcome. He was anxious to lecture the Arab tribesmen he met about the harmless oryx, fast approaching extinction, but there were other, less attractive creatures to come across. The scorpions — none of them deadly, he observed, in what sounds like an attempt to cheer himself up — were quite capable of crippling a strong man for a day or more. Then there were the dust-coloured African puff-adder and the horned viper, whose bite, according to his Arab guide, could best be countered with liberal applications of oryx blood — an interesting dilemma for an ecologically-aware traveller like Fiennes, which it seems he never faced in reality.

Least appealing of all were the spiders of the Nej'd, and least appealing of them, the camel spider, with its large eyes, cruel beak and apparently insatiable appetite for flesh, whether it be that of a camel or a human. With travelling companions like that behind them, the inhospitable but unpeopled sands must have seemed strangely welcoming. Fiennes may even occasionally have thought wistfully while he was in the Nej'd of the communist landmines that had been the only serious danger on his earlier patrols.

The little group spent four days wandering among the dunes, scanning the horizon with their binoculars and noting occasional tracks of men and camels. Thesiger, with his hatred of the internal combustion engine and all its works, would have laughed: on their last day in the desert, they tried to follow the trail of a group of bedu, only to find that the steep dune slopes were too much for their vehicles. The sweat of the Arabs and the wide pads of their camels had outdone the best that western technology could offer.

It is worth noting in passing that the desert Arabs adapted to the motorcar much more successfully than the Arabists did. Fiennes remarked later that, just as the Rashidi had for hundreds of years been the best travellers of the sands on their camels, so in the twentieth century they have proved themselves the most skilful drivers of the four-wheel-drive vehicles that now roar through the desert.

On the trail of the lost city, Fiennes's conclusion was that more, not less, technology was needed. As they hurried back towards the gravel plains in reply to a radio call from the main body of the patrol — 'bouncing and jolting' in a way that would have disgusted the traditional travellers on their camels, and frequently getting stuck in the sand for their pains — he reached a crucial decision. Somehow, the search would have to be made from the air.

In 1970, two years after his first brush with the story of Ubar, Fiennes left Oman, and returned to civilian life in London. There, he intended to make a career as an organiser of sponsored expeditions to the wild and unknown parts of the world. Like the Arab travellers who preceded him, he found that one of the most intractable difficulties of travel, in the Arabian deserts or anywhere else for that matter, was finding someone to pay the bills. In Fiennes's case, he began to look for sponsorship from manufacturers and companies. Everything he took on his expeditions around the world, he decided, would have to be paid for by someone else. Ubar, however, was not a project that attracted sponsors, who were unaccountably anxious to see their products disappearing into the northern snows on high-profile races to the Pole, but not to see them as part of a fully-equipped search of the deserts of Oman.

For the next twenty years, Fiennes heard with anguish of occasional efforts by other people to find the lost city. One, using a hot-air balloon to get the aerial perspective Fiennes himself had already decided was necessary, had based his search at Shis'r, where Fiennes's expedition had paused before.

It was, in a sense, chance that brought him back onto the trail of Ubar. Fiennes had been working for the international businessman and philanthropist Dr Armand Hammer, and through his work came into contact with an American film-maker, Nick Clapp, a man who had been planning for years to make a documentary about Oman and the lost city. Clapp, like Fiennes, had researched his subject avidly, reading widely about modern Arabian exploration, about the ancient frankincense trade and about the tales and legends of Ubar. Significantly, he had also started making inquiries at NASA, the American space agency, about the possibility of using the Challenger space shuttle programme in the search for the city.

His idea — using space infra-red photography to search for clues that might be invisible from the surface, or even lie hidden beneath the sands — appeared to have caught the imagination of the technicians. Specialists from the Jet Propulsion Laboratory in Pasadena, California, spread their net wider, involving other American and French satellite programmes as well. The idea was that space photographs, once interpreted by sophisticated computer technology, could reveal anything which caused the slightest unnatural swelling in the desert sands; information which experienced archaeologists could use to trace buried man-made foundations.

Fiennes and Clapp decided to pool their resources: Fiennes's connections in Muscat, they reasoned, might help them obtain the necessary permission from a sceptical Omani government. But there was a long way to go before they could mount an actual expedition. Fiennes still had to earn a living, and that meant organising more high-profile expeditions for his sponsors. The frozen wastes of the North Pole, rather than the deserts of Oman, beckoned.

While he prepared an attempt to be the first to reach the Pole without outside assistance, the two men continued to correspond about their plans, meeting whenever they could arrange it. The pictures from Challenger and the other satellites had not lived up to Fiennes's wilder hopes: there were no miraculous photographs of a hidden city, mapped out beneath the sands by an all-seeing eye from space. But they did show stretches of the 'desert road' described by Bertram Thomas, together with a mysterious L-shaped feature close to it; by combining pictures made at different wavelengths, by different satellites, it was possible to make out several ancient tracks, deep under the sand dunes. At last there was something concrete to search for and investigate.

Just as important, there was also something specific to show HM Sultan Qaboos, the ruler of Oman, to back up their appeals to be allowed to mount an expedition. The Sultan had already made clear that he would not have Oman turned into some kind of theme-park playground for every archaeologist and adventurer to turn over with picks and shovels, but he was impressed with Fiennes's travels, some of which had benefited from Omani sponsorship. The expedition could go ahead, he said, as long as any digging was carefully controlled.

But it was only after the North Pole expedition had been undertaken — unsuccessfully, as it turned out — that the details of the search for Ubar could be attended to. An initial reconnaissance expedition was mounted, including Fiennes and Clapp, along with an expert archaeologist named Dr Juris Zarins, a scientist from the Jet Propulsion Laboratory, and an American lawyer specialising in fundraising. It was a professionally and scientifically-equipped team that contrasted markedly with the amateurish determination of Thomas, Philby, or Thesiger. Desert exploration, it seemed, had finally reached the twentieth century, leap-frogging the age of the motorcar and arriving in that of the satellite technician and the PR executive.

They had a tight schedule: eight days in which to visit every important archaeological site in southern Oman, following the frankincense trail in the hope that detective work on the ground, coupled with advanced photography from space, might lead them to Ubar. It was a schedule that would have amazed every other traveller who had explored the deserts. Four-wheel-drive vehicles were out of date, let alone camels. They flew by Bell 205 helicopter out of Salalah airbase — one journey from Thamrait to Andhur, which would have taken four hours by jeep and days by camel, whisked by in around thirty minutes. When they landed and needed to check where they were, they did it simply by switching on their electronic position indicator, pushing a few buttons, and then reading off their precise location given by backbearings from three satellites.

The helicopter age, however, did not insulate this expedition from all the problems faced by its predecessors. Local tribesmen were not always welcoming to outsiders, and the ones that Fiennes's team came across were occasionally armed with Kalashnikov rifles rather than the ancient weapons other explorers had faced. On one occasion, a group of Mahra herdsmen near Andhur complained that noise of the expedition's arrival had frightened their goats, causing six of the animals to be crushed to death. The traditions of hospitality held good as they spelled out their complaints over a morning coffee, but it was clear that there would have to be a settlement of some kind. Trouble with the locals would be the surest way to have the permission to dig rescinded by the Omani government.

The solution was much the same as any of the explorers might have reached. Claims for twelve hundred rials were whittled down by bargaining to two hundred and a few items of clothing.

Satellite navigation was one thing, but modern technology could not always guarantee the exactitude of the measurements the team was making. The height of sand-dunes in the desert, like the length of fish that wriggle off a line, tends to increase as the stories are told, and Fiennes admits that even his highly-qualified team was not immune from exaggeration. Dunes of around two hundred feet seemed to grow mysteriously in the reportage until they towered over six hundred feet in height. With that phenomenon, at least, Harry St John Philby might have sympathised.

There was disappointment early on in the expedition, when the team reached the mysterious L-shaped depression that had seemed so promising. It took the space scientist and the archaeologist very little time to agree that the site was nothing more than an ancient lake-bed. The search seemed to be back at square one.

But there were still the newly-revealed camel-tracks to be investigated, and the team moved away from the plains, the mountains, and the Nej'd, back to the edge of the sands where Fiennes had searched years before. Once again, he was back in the region of Shis'r and Fasad.

The countryside had changed in the twenty years that had passed: it was almost an image of the wider transformation to Arabia that Thesiger had lamented earlier. Where once there had been barren desert, houses had sprung up — a modern Arab-style development at Shis'r, for instance, designed to tempt the nomadic Arabs with the benefits of agriculture and a settled life.

Shis'r had been the base for several searches for Ubar. Fiennes himself had paused briefly there to inspect the ruined fort; Thesiger and Thomas had both visited the site; the hot-air balloonist who had mounted his own Ubar expedition had based himself at the water-hole there; and now Fiennes and his team did the same. Here was a source of sweet water close to the edge of the barren sands of the Empty Quarter: it must have been attractive to the ancient frankincense caravans as a staging post hole on their route north for the same reasons as the searchers had chosen it. Shis'r was added to the list of sites to be investigated in more detail when the expedition returned the following spring.

At this stage, it did not look hopeful. Dr Zarins was frank in his assessment: "I do know there is nothing in the Rub Al Khali. We have done the reconnaissance, and have nothing to show for it," he said. There were a few shards of pottery from round about the Shis'r site. Otherwise, the expedition had drawn a blank.

The report which went to the Omani government and to the sponsors of the expedition was less outspoken. Whatever happened, Fiennes had to maintain the confidence of his sponsors, or they would pull their money out. "It is not impossible that Shis'r may turn out to be the mythical Ubar," the sponsors were told. It seemed more like a wish than a realistic assessment.

The invasion of Kuwait caused a few months' delay, but by the autumn of 1991, the team had gathered again in Muscat, ready for their final effort. Descriptions of their preparations point up once again the contrast with the traditional explorers. They wanted cloth napkins to eat their meals with, they told their sponsors; paper ones for a four-month expedition would be a shocking waste of space and resources. And of course, to prevent infections spreading among the party, there would have to be individual rings to keep the napkins in… They were also provided with a portable telephone to keep them in touch with civilisation — even an escort from the Omanis' Special Task Force, which was able to ease their way with the traffic police.

The reaction of Thesiger to the suggestion that he should have started each meal under the desert sky with a napkin carefully spread on his lap, or that he should check in by telephone as he sat on a lonely dune can only be imagined.

Exactly why and when Fiennes and his friends fixed on Shis'r as the site of Ubar is far from clear. The members of the team themselves disagree. Nick Clapp, the cameraman, claims that satellite images showed a network of old tracks converging on the region, and so gave the vital clue, while Fiennes and the archaeologist Zarins maintain they treated Shis'r only as a convenient base. Dr Zarins, according to Fiennes, said later, with commendable honesty: "I didn't think Shis'r was Ubar even when we started digging there."

Every authority they had checked, from Thomas and Thesiger to the Omani tribesmen they spoke to, seemed to bear that assessment out. Nobody believed that the ruins of Shis'r were more than three hundred years old. After a few weeks of digging, though, it was clear that the pile of rubble they had first seen went back much further than that. Some of the artefacts that were turned up seemed to date from the Greek and Roman periods — the very time that Ubar, if it had gained prosperity from the frankincense trade, would have been at its peak. Later finds of pottery and glass from Aden, Syria and even China showed how important a trading centre it was.

Out of the rubble there gradually emerged the clear outline of a ruined tower, with a wall connecting it to a second circular tower and a third horseshoe-shaped fortification. There were, too, clues to the natural disaster that might have engulfed it. The archaeologist Zarins suggested that the earth may literally have fallen away under the central area of the fortification, perhaps because of the sinking of the water table, or possibly even because of an earthquake.

The site the team had uncovered was small — around the size of a football pitch, according to Fiennes — but they reckoned there would have been nowhere of anything like the same size for hundreds of miles around. It was easy to see how the legend of a lost city might have arisen.

Gradually, the work pressed on. By the end of January, barely a month after the start of the dig, they had revealed nine towers, most of the main outer wall, and six thousand or so individual artefacts. Still, perhaps, there was no incontrovertible evidence to say that this was the site of Ubar. But they had found enough to justify Fiennes's account of his audience in Sultan Qaboos's majlis.

"'Is it definitely Ubar,' he asked me," he says in *Atlantis of the Sands*, his account of the expedition.

"'I believe so, Your Majesty. It is difficult to know what else it could be.'"

Not everyone, of course, accepted the identification of Shis'r with Ubar; experts in other countries still press the claims of other sites. But even if Shis'r is not positively identified as this lost city, it is undeniably a lost city. The discovery gave a tantalising glimpse of a world of bustling prosperity hundreds of years ago on the fringes of the desert.

The search that found it was not in any sense a classic Arabian journey in the tradition of the great desert explorers, but perhaps it showed the way that the challenges of the Empty Quarter may be met in the future.

Thesiger himself observed that he used camels because they were the best form of transport available: crossing the desert by camel when cars were available would be no more than a stunt. He would not be interested in stunts like that, and Fiennes certainly was not. He puts his success down quite unashamedly to luck, hard work, archaeological instinct — plus generous sponsors and a wide variety of technical aids.

In all this, the desert explorers of the twentieth century have much in common with the merchants and traders who preceded them centuries ago. The men who organised the frankincense caravans upon which the wealth of Ubar was founded relied on their skill, courage and vision; but they were businessmen, not explorers or adventurers. They would certainly not have scorned any aid that could have helped them achieve their object. Perhaps it is fitting that the men who came centuries later in search of what they left behind should have taken the same pragmatic view of their quest.

THE GATHERING DUSK

"They are all gone, these great ones... Can the sorry little crowd of us today be in the tradition, even? I fear not."

– T E Lawrence

Thesiger's, then, was the last of the great traditional journeys of exploration across the Empty Quarter. It is hard to imagine a traveller feeling the same sense of unity with his harsh surroundings when he sits encapsulated inside a four-wheel-drive, with an air-conditioning unit sifting the dust from the desert winds, and a portable telephone clipped reassuringly to his dashboard.

The desert travellers of the past were seldom alone — one thing on which they all agree is that the sand forced them into a companionship closer than anything they could find in the world outside — but their world was bounded by the harsh landscape, the patient camels, and the ever-present threat of thirst and disaster.

Today, though, the oil companies have mapped vast areas of what used to be unknown land. Even where there are no roads, aircraft and satellites criss-cross the desert, and flashing lights in the sky remind the traveller that he has come from softer, more comfortable world.

And yet, there is an irony in the quotation which starts this chapter. Perhaps the modern travellers — the "sorry little crowd of us today" — have no hope of being considered in the great tradition of Arabian explorers. But the fact that it was Lawrence himself who asked that question suggests that the answer is less simple and less final than he supposed.

If Lawrence, with his military expedition alongside Feisal, changed the nature of the tradition, he still showed much the same courage and iron will as those who went before him. If Fiennes relied on satellite navigation systems, helicopters, and every technological aid a modern world could supply, he still needed the same imagination and the same belief in his own intuition that explorers have shown since the days when the first spice caravans set off into the sands.

The impetus that drove Thesiger and the travellers before him into the desert — the search for something timeless, something within themselves — has survived.

And once the engine is turned off and the car is hidden in the shadows, perhaps even a modern traveller can detect the faintest scent of what the explorers felt in the liquid blackness of a desert night.

ACKNOWLEDGEMENTS

Most of the explorers whose journeys are described here are now far beyond the reach of would-be interviewers: one who was not was Wilfred Thesiger, and I am extremely grateful for having had the chance to meet and interview him during one of his visits to the Emirates.

Much of the book was written when I was living in Dubai, and I have many debts of gratitude to friends in England who helped with research. Mrs Jessica Taylor put her encyclopaedic knowledge of classical civilisations at my disposal, and spent many long and arduous hours in Leeds University Library on research, not just into the ancient history of the Arabian peninsula, but into scores of apparently unrelated problems and queries. Similarly, my good friend Miss Pippa McCarthy helped with her investigations in London into the burial of Sir Richard Burton.

The illustrations are individually acknowledged, but Brian MacDermot, Chairman of London's Mathaf Gallery, was especially helpful. The staff of the Bodleian Library, Oxford were also extremely co-operative, whether in handling requests sent by letter from four thousand miles away, or in dealing with an anxious author in the library itself. My thanks also go to the National Portrait Gallery and the Royal Geographical Society for supplying further illustrations.

It was, of course, living in Dubai which first sparked my interest in the Arab world, and for five fulfilling years there, I should thank all my friends at Dubai Television — in particular, because they originally gave me the chance to work in the Gulf, His Highness Sheikh Hasher Maktoum, Mr Nasib Bitar, and Mr Riyad Shuaibi. Also in Dubai, my friend Chuck Grieve, at Motivate Publishing, who edited the book.

Finally, thanks to Philips Middle East, without whose sponsorship support publication of this book would not have been possible.

BIBLIOGRAPHY

Asher, Michael, *Thesiger — A Biography*, Viking, London; Motivate Publishing, Dubai 1994

Blunt, Lady Anne, *A Pilgrimage to Nejd*, John Murray, 1881

Burckhardt, J L, *Travels in Arabia*, London 1829

Browning, Iain, *Petra*, Chatto and Windus 1989

Burgyne, Elizabeth (ed), *Gertrude Bell from her Personal Papers*, Benn, 1958

Burton, Sir Richard, *Personal Narrative of a Pilgrimage to El-Medina and Mecca*, London 1885

Dictionary of National Biography

Doe, Brian, *Southern Arabia*, Thames & Hudson 1971

Doughty, Charles, *Travels in Arabia Deserta*, Cambridge University Press 1888

Farwell, Byron, *Burton — A Biography of Sir Richard Francis Burton*, Penguin 1990

Fiennes, Ranulph, *Atlantis of the Sands*, Bloomsbury, 1992

Garnett, David (ed), *The Essential T E Lawrence*, Oxford University Press 1992

Hakluyt, *Voyages*, London 1863

Lawrence, T E, *Seven Pillars of Wisdom*, Jonathan Cape, London 1935

Longford, Elizabeth, *A Pilgrimage of Passion — The Life of Wilfrid Scawen Blunt*, Weidenfield and Nicholson, London 1979

MEED, *UAE, a MEED Practical Guide*, 1990

Palgrave, W G, *Personal Narrative of a Year's Journey Through Central and Eastern Arabia*, Macmillan, London 1865

Philby, H St J, *The Empty Quarter*, Constable, London 1933

— *Heart of Arabia*, Constable, London 1922

Piepenburg, Fritz, *New Travellers' Guide to Yemen*, Yemen Tourism Co. 1987

Pliny, *Natural History*, III–VII Loeb Classical Library

Trench, Richard, *Arabian Travellers*, Macmillan 1986

Thesiger, Wilfred, *Arabian Sands*, Longmans, Green and Co. 1959; Motivate Publishing, Dubai 1994

— *The Marsh Arabs*, London 1964; Motivate Publishing, Dubai 1994

— *The Life of My Choice*, London 1987

Thomas, Bertram, *Arabia Felix*, Jonathan Cape, London 1932

— *The Arabs*, Thornton Butterworth 1937

Wellsted, J R, *Travels in Arabia*, London 1838

Wilson, Jeremy, *Lawrence of Arabia*, Heinemann 1989

Winstone, H V F, *Gertrude Bell*, Constable, London 1978

INDEX